AN INTRODUCTION TO
PHILOSOPHY

AN INTRODUCTION TO
PHILOSOPHY

By

W. A. SINCLAIR

LECTURER IN PHILOSOPHY IN THE
UNIVERSITY OF EDINBURGH

OXFORD UNIVERSITY PRESS

LONDON   NEW YORK   TORONTO

CONTENTS

PREFACE

THIS book has been written for those who say, as so many do, 'Can you tell me of an introductory book on philosophy? I don't want anything technical or learned. I just want to find out what philosophy is.'

It therefore assumes that the reader is interested either in philosophy or in satisfying himself whether philosophy is or is not worth studying, but it presupposes no previous knowledge of the subject whatever.

This book, like a series of broadcasts with a similar purpose which the B.B.C. in 1942 asked me to give, is based on the manuscript of some of the introductory chapters of a larger book on theory of knowledge and kindred matters, on which I had been working for some years up to the outbreak of war and had then to leave uncompleted. This manuscript is called *The Owl of Minerva*, as the bird of the Goddess of Wisdom provides a convenient label.

What I have tried to do with this owlet from that nest is to bring the reader to a position in which he knows, from his own experience in working through the book, what it feels like to think philosophically, and from which he can go forward to reading the greater philosophers for himself with some hope of profiting from direct acquaintance with those majestic and regrettably inaccessible minds.

If this book should, as a by-product, help any reader to achieve a tolerable working philosophy for himself on those aspects of the human situation with which it deals, so much the better. That, however, is not its primary purpose. It is meant to introduce, and at the end is some advice as to the lines on which further reading might most rewardingly go.

W. A. S.

26 *May* 1944

CHAPTER I

What Philosophers do, and why they do it

HERE we are, in this complicated world. We did not make it; we find ourselves in it. We have to make shift as best we can to survive in it, to enjoy being alive in it among our fellows, and, if we can, to improve those parts of it over which we have any control or influence. We must therefore try to understand it at least well enough to enable us to regulate our lives with competence.

The attempt to understand the universe and ourselves and our place in the universe, whether for theoretical interest or for material practical purposes, is philosophy. We are all therefore inevitably philosophers in so far as we all have to have some views about the universe and our place in it. These may be very naïve views, but they are philosophical views none the less. Even the disgruntled young man who says 'Women are all the same' is expressing a philosophical view about the social structure with special reference to one half of the human race and its allegedly disappointing behaviour therein. It is customary not to call such casual views 'philosophical', and to restrict that title to views seriously meditated upon in quiet hours and held as considered conclusions, but this distinction is at bottom only a distinction between simple-minded philosophies and comparatively better considered ones. An 'introduction to philosophy' is therefore a first attempt at getting a somewhat better understanding than we at present have of ourselves and of the universe and of our place in it.

This can be an intellectual adventure. If the reader is willing, it may result in his coming to look at things in an entirely new and fresh way, in a way he had never thought of before. Studying philosophy is not merely learning one more subject. Philosophy is not in fact a subject that can be learned, as algebra or French grammar can be learned. Studying philosophy does not mean learning a number of new facts. There is in it, of course, a certain amount of the learning of new facts, but the main part consists in learning to look at the old and familiar facts in a new and fresh way.

This cannot be expected to come about without effort. It requires a good deal from both the writer and the reader. It requires me to use language, which is a system of conventional symbols developed in the remote past for very different and more obvious purposes, to draw the reader's attention to certain matters which are very far from obvious and are sometimes difficult to understand ; and it requires the reader to make the effort of doing some hard thinking on his own. Neither I nor anybody else can *teach* him philosophy. The student of philosophy must shift for himself.

There is another fact also which makes philosophy a subject that cannot be taught. In most other subjects, such as chemistry or biology or even history, there is a common body of doctrine upon which all who are concerned with the advancement and propagation of the subject are agreed. Upon points labelled as ' controversial ' they may differ, but upon the main lines they are in agreement, at least as far as the introduction to the subject is concerned. In philosophy, on the other hand, there is no such general agreement. What I write here is therefore only what I think about the matter. It is not necessarily what other philosophers think ; and when we disagree, I cannot maintain that I am right and that the others are wrong. The most I can say is that what I write is the way in which the matters in question appear to me. It is probable that most contemporary philosophers would agree on the whole with the substance of the first five chapters, but by no means all of them would agree with chapters VI to X. Many of them would say that in these later chapters I have perversely gone wrong, while I should say that to think as they do seems curiously remote to me now. In other words, we none of us know. We are each doing the best we can, but none of us is entitled to claim authority, and none of us, except the more popular and negligible, presumes to do so. The reader must therefore bear in mind throughout that what I write has not necessarily any consensus of educated opinion behind it.

I should like to add ' as yet ', but this would merely indicate my belief that the outline given in the later chapters, inevitably sketchy though it be, approximates to the line on which the philosophical development of the immediate future will proceed, and that until it does so proceed much of the present inhibiting confusion in philosophy and in many subjects on the borderland of philosophy will unnecessarily persist. In this belief I may be wrong, and the reader at his present stage is therefore advised to regard what I write as serving primarily to introduce him to the subject and to make reasonably clear what is the sort of problem upon which he must thereafter exercise his own judgement.

Let us then turn to the first stage of a serious attempt to understand this world in which we find ourselves. When we set ourselves to this, numbers of facts emerge which are very confusing. This world of ours turns out to be a most astonishing world. All sorts of extremely queer things happen in it. This, presumably, everybody knows, or at least realizes when it is brought to his attention, but few people realize that some of the queerest and most astonishing facts are the facts concerned in how we know, and how we understand. This is the point at which we begin to think together philosophically. We have begun to deal with philosophical questions, and we straightway light on the perhaps surprising point that if we start seriously trying to understand the world, we find ourselves having to try first to understand what we are doing when we understand. The facts show us that we cannot go on taking the processes of knowing and understanding for granted. They turn out to be very remarkable when we think about them.

This becomes clearer if we notice that there is one respect, among others, in which philosophical questions are somewhat peculiar. With most questions, we need not trouble ourselves about the answer until the question has been asked. If for instance I were to ask ' Was this book lying on its side, or was it upright in a bookcase, before you picked it up to read it ? ', then the answer to that question was of no importance or interest, either to you or to me or to anybody else, before I asked the question. There are, however, some kinds of questions which are different, because we have assumed answers to them before it ever occurred to us to ask the questions, and even if we never ask them. Questions about the nature of the universe, and about man and his place in the universe—philosophical questions—are of this kind. As we shall see later, questions of this apparently odd kind are very important—they are of great *practical* importance—but at the moment we are concerned only with the surprising fact that we have assumed answers to them before we even thought of asking them.

Take an example. Think of the question whether time can be measured independently of space. This is as abstruse and remote a question as one could well conceive, and it is not a question that anyone is likely to ask unprompted. But, even though we may never have thought of asking this question, we have assumed an answer to it. We have *assumed* that time can be measured independently of space, as is shown for instance by our taking it for granted that if a wireless concert lasts for thirty-five minutes in the studio in London it will last for thirty-five minutes when listened to in Manchester and Australia. Most readers will feel inclined to reply that this is the only answer that could be assumed. It is, however, not the only answer. There are innumerable other answers that could be assumed. For instance, an astronomer investigating the stars and planets would assume a different answer. He does not think that time can be measured in the same way everywhere. According to the astronomers and astrophysicists, if we start inquiring into questions of the measurement of time where vast spaces are concerned, we find very queer and astonishing things—things that seem queer and astonishing only because they do not make sense on the assumptions we have unconsciously made. If for instance I tap my pen on the little iron cross-bar of the folding table at which I am now writing, then at the instant at which I tapped my pen, an event of some kind or other occurred in, say, the Pole Star. The two events were, we say, simultaneous. That is to say, they were simultaneous as measured by us. And away at the other side of the known universe, say in the star Arcturus, some other event occurred which also was simultaneous with the tapping of my pen here. Yet, that event in Arcturus may have occurred long before, or long after, the event in the Pole Star, as measured by anyone on either of those stars.

This seems queer and indeed impossible to us, simply because we have assumed one answer among the many possible ones to the apparently remote and abstruse question whether time can be measured independently of space. Somebody else, who had assumed a different answer, would find those happenings in Arcturus and the Pole Star in no way out of the ordinary.

Now let us take an example of an assumption of a different kind. In winter we expect that spring will duly come, as it did last year and in previous years. We so confidently expect to see the young grass growing and the leaves coming out on the trees that it never occurs to us to expect anything else. We have assumed that the seasons will regularly recur. We have assumed a certain uniformity in nature. What justification have we for assuming it? It is no justification to say that spring always comes. That is merely to repeat the assertion. It does not explain why we are justified in expecting spring to come. This view that the seasons recur regularly is an assumption we have made without noticing that it is an assumption.[1]

This assumption is made by you and me, but it is not made by everybody. There are many human beings in remoter areas of the earth who do not make such an assumption. Many primitive tribes to-day, like primitive peoples in the past, do not believe that spring will come inevitably after winter, and harvest after seed-time. They think that spring will not come at all, unless they themselves do something to make it come. They therefore put themselves to considerable trouble and inconvenience in carrying out various rites and ceremonies which they believe will entice or compel spring to come. Towards the end of next winter, the Hopi Indians in Arizona, for instance, and many other tribes more remote from civilization than they, will set about the magical proceedings which they consider necessary to bring spring and summer, and to make the crops sprout and grow to harvesting maturity. In the same way they believe that the seasons of the present year are

[1] There is a justification for assuming it. This will be discussed later in chapter IX.

coming in due order only because of the ceremonies they carried out at the tail end of last winter.

The relevant difference between those primitive tribesmen and ourselves is that we have made a certain assumption about the succession of the seasons, and they have made no such assumption. They have made a very different assumption. The tribesmen of course never posed to themselves the articulate question : ' Is there an immutable natural law of a regular seasonal succession due to the gyrations of this planet on an inclined axis in an elliptical orbit about the sun? Or do the seasonal changes come only because we and our medicine men compel them to come by our spring-time magical rites ? ' They did not ask themselves that question, nor, I expect, did you ; but you are working on the assumption that there is such an inevitable natural succession and that these magical rites are of no effect, while the primitive tribesmen are working on the assumption that there is no such natural succession and that these magical rites are potent and essential.

The purpose of quoting the preceding examples is to bring out as clearly as possible the two fundamental points with which we are here concerned. These are, first, that we have all made assumptions on general and apparently abstruse matters, and second, that we are seldom clearly conscious that we have made them. Let us take these two points in turn.

As to the first, it comes out quite clearly that we have all made many quite definite assumptions about very general questions, such as the nature of time, the nature of the laws governing the succession of the seasons, and the like. Further, our particular actions and our particular opinions on particular points are what they are because those general assumptions are what they are. If those general assumptions had been different, then our particular actions and particular opinions on particular points would be different. We could not intelligibly say to a friend who has kept us waiting: 'You are late', unless we and the friend had both assumed that time can be measured in the same way at different places, at least when places close together on the surface of the earth are concerned. A farmer could not plan the working of his farm as he does, unless he assumed that the succession of the seasons was regular and dependable.

We lie at the mercy of these assumptions. If they are sound assumptions, well and good. If they are not sound, we are involved in misunderstanding, inconvenience, and, in extreme cases, gross failure. The farmer's assumptions about the seasonal succession appear to be sound, and he therefore runs his farm effectively and produces food. The primitive tribesman on the other hand, who has made assumptions that we consider unsound about the succession of the seasons, is put to a great deal of unproductive labour and trouble every year in carrying out complicated magical rites, on which he would not waste his time if he were to rid himself of his unsound assumptions. If there is something unsound in our underlying assumptions, then we are not only involved in misunderstanding, but also suffer very serious practical disadvantages.

The second point which emerges is that we are seldom clearly aware of what our underlying assumptions are. Striking instances of this occasionally occur among those who pride themselves on being practical men. Many of the opinions of such men are without doubt based on practical experience, but many others of their opinions are not so, being based instead on highly speculative hypotheses unverified by experience. Such men are seldom aware of this, and sincerely believe that all their

opinions are based on practical experience. Discussion with them is in consequence somewhat irregular in its progress. This phenomenon occurs frequently in any highly institutionalized human society, as for instance the medical profession or the Army.

To make ourselves clearly aware of our underlying assumptions involves painstaking mental labour. In other words, it involves some hard philosophical thinking. But until we do this, and make ourselves clear, as far as we can, as to what underlying assumptions we have in fact made, we remain subject to them, and to all the consequences they entail. It is therefore not at all an exaggeration to say that until we have discovered what our underlying assumptions are, we are not free either in thinking or in acting, because all our particular opinions, and those of our particular actions that are consequent upon our opinions, are such that they are confined within the limits set by these unrecognized assumptions.

It turns out therefore that the common belief about the relation in which our general or philosophical views or assumptions stand to our particular opinions and actions is the wrong way round. The common belief is that all men have as their first care to cope with the practical difficulties of life, and that they do this more or less successfully according to their fortunes and capacities without entangling themselves in metaphysics, while some few among them, so it is believed, who happen to have the interest and the necessary leisure, may if they wish go on to raise questions of a philosophical nature and to attempt the answering of them, while all this time the vast remaining majority of mankind go about their business without troubling to answer or even to ask such questions, and without being any the worse for either of these omissions. This belief is an inversion of the facts.

It is of course the case that conscious and deliberate inquiry into topics of this kind, such as we are now attempting, is undertaken only at a comparatively late and leisured stage, and cannot be undertaken except in such conditions ; but, whether a man is aware of it or not, what he thinks, or ' has unrecognized in the back of his mind ' about those apparently remote and unpractical topics sets limits within which he is confined in his thinking about everything else. When, if ever, a man reaches that later stage of conscious and deliberate inquiry, he is disturbed to discover just what are the unrecognized presuppositions which have thus been governing his life and limiting the work done in it.

As might be expected, the assumptions we have unconsciously made turn out on investigation to be mostly unsatisfactory. They are muddled, fluctuating and inadequate, and we move from one to another without noticing it. It therefore requires painstaking intellectual labour to make ourselves clearly aware of what these assumptions are, and it then requires further intellectual labour to examine and appraise them and, where necessary and possible, amend them into something better. This is what the work of philosophers is. It is very difficult work and philosophers do not pretend to be very good at it, but it is being done. This is the sort of work the reader is himself doing at this moment, by reading this book and thinking along with me as I write.

This is the most arduous of all intellectual pursuits, and there is nothing discreditable in finding it somewhat strange and difficult. Socrates and Plato and David Hume and Kant and all the great philosophers found it difficult too, and somewhat ruefully confessed as much. A man cannot have a ' flair ' for philosophy as he can for, say, mathematics. There are mathematical geniuses to whom mathematics comes easy. There are not, in that sense of the word,

philosophical geniuses. Philosophy is only common sense laboriously pursued. To study philosophy is to persist in carrying on common sense inquiry beyond the point at which it becomes difficult, the point at which most people abandon the attempt.

Before going on to this attempt, there is a general reservation on the preceding that has to be made and kept in mind. The reader will note that we have here discussed as examples only assumptions which readily become clear to us when our attention is drawn to them, even though we are at first unconscious of making them. No doubt if human beings were mere intellects, without feelings and emotions, all our assumptions would become clear to us when once our attention had been drawn to them. But we are not mere intellects, and in many cases our assumptions are such that to recognize them and bring them to consciousness would give us a most unpleasant emotional shock. In such cases it is difficult or impossible for us to make ourselves conscious of our underlying assumptions by any ordinary conscious introspective effort. Some special technique, of which as yet philosophers and psychologists would claim only the beginnings of an understanding, is required. We shall return to this matter in chapter X, but in the meantime shall proceed in our study without raising the complex issues involved in examining the effect of our emotions and feelings upon our opinions and assumptions. This does not mean that any adequate understanding of the situation is possible without some such inquiry. It only means that the best way to reach such an understanding is to make this inquiry at a later stage.

CHAPTER II

Knowing About Knowing

PHILOSOPHICAL inquiry consists largely in finding out first what are the assumptions or presuppositions we have made, without being clearly aware of having done so,[1] then in examining them, and thereafter in amending them where possible into something better.

How are we to do this? To sit down and think the matter out for ourselves is an admirable ambition, but people who make the attempt soon find that it cannot be done. It is too difficult. If you have tried thinking out on your own the problems of the nature of time touched on in the previous chapter, you have probably found that the more you went on inquiring, the more confused you became. There is nothing discreditable to your intellectual capacities in this. It happens to everybody.

What then are we to do in order to lay bare our misleading presuppositions, get rid of them, and find better ones? We can do this only by taking advantage of the previous labour of others. That labour is the service given to their kind by many generations of thoughtful men, the philosophers. If a man reads the greater philosophical writings, he finds that he is not merely accumulating new information about the opinions held by the eminent thinkers of past generations. He has a different kind of experience. He finds that something is happening to him. He finds that he is changing the way in which he himself looks at things. He finds, when he has read one of the greater philosophers, that he has not been

[1] This is what G. W. F. Hegel (1770–1831, very influential German philosopher) meant by his saying ' The Owl of Minerva takes not its flight till the shades of night have fallen.'

engaged only in intellectual antiquarianism. He finds that his outlook and habit of mind have changed in the process. He may indeed be surprised on subsequent meditation to observe how much they have changed.

This is the reason for studying the greater philosophers. It is a thoroughly practical reason. It makes a man different from what he was before. It makes him better able to understand this queer and puzzling world, in so far as we can ever hope to understand it. For a man who takes it, this experience is, and feels, an intellectual adventure. He feels that he has made a step forward into a fresh world, or, to speak not in metaphor but more exactly, he feels that he has come to look at the old world in a fresh way. Moreover, if he once comes to see it in this fresh way, he never goes back. Philosophy is not something a man can learn and then forget. When he has once acquired a fresher and more adequate understanding, he does not go back to an earlier and more unsophisticated one.

In the next few chapters an account is given of some of the changes that would happen to you if you started on a reasonably well-guided course of reading in the greater philosophers. Such reading requires guidance. A man cannot pick up a book by some famous philosopher, read it, and expect to profit by doing so. Philosophical books are difficult to find one's way about in, and if a man tries dipping into philosophy here and there as famous names may attract him, he may be titillated at first, but he soon becomes confused and discouraged.

The reason is that no one philosopher can be understood, considered by himself. Different philosophies are not independent of each other and merely different. No philosopher is adequately intelligible without reference to his predecessors. No philosopher starts afresh, even though he may announce himself as doing so and quite sincerely believe himself to be doing so, as was the manner of philosophers some centuries ago. Like the rest of us, every philosopher grew up from boyhood having in the back of his mind those assumptions which were common to the society in which he lived. When he started the serious study of philosophy, his views and assumptions were altered by contact with his philosophical predecessors, as you are beginning to have yours altered by your present inquiry. He further changed his views for himself, by independent work on what he had thus inherited, thereby producing in the end his own characteristic philosophy, which then in its turn acted as an influence upon the generations of his successors, including you and me. If therefore you attempt to read any one of the great philosophers by himself alone, the effect will be merely puzzling, and will almost certainly produce as a consequence the impression that the great man's preoccupations were somewhat footling. If, however, you read the greater philosophers in something like chronological order, you will find that the views of each appear not puzzling or footling, but impressively plain common sense, as being what any thoughtful man of great clarity of mind and great vigour of application, e.g. yourself, would have concluded in the circumstances.

Further, not only do the views of successive generations seem reasonable to us when studied in this way, but we also find that our own views are developing from day to day along much the same lines as those on which the views of our predecessors had developed from generation to generation. We find that we are ourselves passing in a short space of time through the main stages of philosophical development through which our forbears had laboriously struggled over many generations. This does not of course apply to minor points, but it does hold of the main stages of philosophical understanding, up to fairly recent times. (In very recent times, of course, the similarity of development ceases, because we cannot detect any commonly accepted development in philosophical thought which our private development can recapitulate, as there is no consensus of educated opinion.)

If therefore you were to set about studying the fundamental problems of philosophy in a serious and systematic way, your experience would be something more or less like what I am now going on to describe.

We have seen that many of our opinions and many of our actions are what they are because of certain views or presuppositions which we have assumed without being at all clear that we have done so. When we first turn our attention to these presuppositions, notice that they exist, and attempt to examine them, our first impression is that there are great numbers of them, apparently unrelated to one another. You have, for instance, assumed that time is of a certain character, and that you are the same person to-day that you were last year—a very remarkable and thought-provoking assumption by the way—and that the seasons will duly recur, and so forth. All these assumptions appear at first to be an unsystematized collection, unrelated one to another. On further inquiry, however, we begin to detect some order or pattern in them. This is the same sort of experience as we have in e.g. learning chemistry. At first, all chemical substances seem to be merely different, and to form a mere collection in which we cannot see any system. But, as we learn more about chemistry, and about chemical families and groups, we are increasingly impressed by the comparative simplicity of the pattern we learn to detect in all the apparent confusion.

In much the same way, we find that these various assumptions we have all made turn out to be not at all higgledy-piggledy, as they once appeared. We begin to detect some system and order in them. We find that some of them are very important; for they affect a great deal. Others are not so important; for they affect much less. Others again are hardly important at all, for they affect very little. There seems to be a sort of range of them, a hierarchy of them, a sort of pyramid of ranks of them, from the unimportant at the bottom to the most important at the top, with innumerable grades of varying degrees of importance ranged between.

By this time our discussion has become much too abstract. Let us take a concrete example. Suppose you and I both happen to be visiting friends somewhere or other, and suppose I think that the last bus leaves at 10.15, and you think that the last bus leaves at 11.15. (It does not for the moment matter *why* we think these things. Let us for the moment accept it that we do.) You can see how in consequence my opinions and actions on all matters connected with getting home are going to be different from yours. When you think there is still time for another game, or for a continued leisurely chat by the fireside, or whatever it be that you are doing, I shall think there is not time, and you will still be comfortably seated, when I have put on my coat and gone to the bus stop. That is, my belief about the time the last bus leaves is going to affect all my opinions and all my actions in this one small slice of my life, namely, catching the bus. My belief lays down limits within which my opinions and actions concerning the bus will fall. The same holds of you. Because your belief is different, your opinions and actions will be different, as far as catching the bus is concerned.

But my belief about the time the bus leaves on a particular evening does not affect my opinions and actions in other departments of life. It has no effect on my opinions about cooking, or poetry, or polar exploration. The range of my opinions and actions that are affected by my assumption about the time the last bus leaves is quite small. If I have made a mistake about the bus time, then the consequences will be inconvenient, and in that sense my assumption is important, but it is not important in the sense of affecting my opinions on a wide range of other matters.

Now let us take an instance of an assumption that has a much wider range. Suppose you fall into conversation with two men, one of whom is a trained lawyer, while the other is a man who has never made any study of law. These two men will be distinguishably different in some ways. In the first place the lawyer will be familiar with numbers of Acts of Parliament, Rules of Court, Common Law precedents, and so forth, most of which the other man will never have heard of. But that will not be the only difference. As you discuss things with them, you will be struck by the fact that the lawyer has an outlook, a way of looking at things, that is peculiarly his own. You will notice that he has the lawyer's characteristic outlook and habit of mind. He has an outlook on all legal and similar matters which is distinguishably different from the ordinary citizen's. This ' comes out ', as we say, whenever you discuss any relevant particular point with him. Suppose there is a dispute about a Will, in consequence of which it looks as if some one member of the dead man's family were going to be unjustly treated if the Will were interpreted rigidly according to the statutes and decisions about Wills. The ordinary private citizen would almost certainly say, probably with heat and indignation, that the statutes ought not to be applied rigidly to this case, while the lawyer in a more even voice would say that they ought to be so applied. The lawyer would agree that the case was hard, but, he would add, if we relax the law in one case, because it happens to be a hard case, the result would be general insecurity, which in the end causes much greater injustice to much larger numbers of people. (This is what lawyers mean by their old saying that 'hard cases make bad law'. Attempting to rectify an individual injustice by disregarding the law means more injustice in the long run.)

You would find that the lawyer has this characteristic attitude on all legal matters. A lawyer does not usually talk about it, but you notice it in his individual opinions and actions on all legal and social matters. If this attitude of his were different, then all his opinions and actions on matters within its range would be different—as they are in fact different in the case of that other man who has a different attitude.

In the same way as my assumption or attitude about the time the last bus leaves affects all my opinions and actions on matters within its range, so the lawyer's professional attitude or outlook affects all his opinions and actions on matters within its range—only in this legal case the range is very much wider. It includes not merely small slices of life, such as catching a bus on one particular evening; it includes all political, social, and similar matters, not only in the lawyer's own life but in the life of the community of which he is a member.

But even this attitude, though its range is so much wider, has its limits. The lawyer's legal habit of mind does not affect his opinions on biology, or on quadratic equations, or on manuring carrots. The same holds of the other man's outlook. It lays down limits within which his opinions and actions on legal and similar points must fall, but it has no effect on his opinions about brass bands or mountain climbing.

We could go on taking examples of assumptions we make which have increasingly wider and more comprehensive ranges of influence. We could draw up a long list of instances, beginning with those that affect comparatively little, like that concerning the bus time, then wider ones like the characteristic legal one, and then still wider and more comprehensive ones, until we reach those that have the widest and most comprehensive range of all. What would you expect these last to be?

The attitudes or assumptions that have the widest and most comprehensive range are our attitudes and presuppositions about the nature of knowledge, about what happens when we know or understand anything.

It may seem odd at first to speak of views and presuppositions about the nature of knowing. It seems more natural to think that knowing is just knowing, and that this is all there is about it. The situation is however very far from being so simple. Consider what is happening when we all look at the same thing. This appears simple, but it is not so. The situation turns out to be remarkably complicated, and exceedingly queer. You look at a pillar-box; you see it is red. You look at the grass; you see it is green. You look at the overcast sky; and you see that the clouds are grey. There is nothing remarkable so far in this; but there exist a fair number of men and a small number of women who are slightly different from you in the eyes, people whom we choose to call 'colour-blind', and they see clouds and grass and pillar-box as indistinguishable in colour.

I remember vividly my own astonishment when I first realised this. I was fishing with a student friend, who was an extremely skilful fisherman and could catch trout when nobody else could touch a fish. We used to walk along the bank of the stream, or the edge of the loch, and he would watch the flies swarming up and down and settling on the water. He would catch one of them, and he would then open his fly-book and compare this natural fly with his collection of artificial flies. He would carefully select one that looked the same, or nearly the same. He then tied it on his line, and cast it, and he generally hooked a trout. One day when he was doing this, I noticed that he selected a teal and red, i.e. a fly with a grey teal feather and a red body. He was about to tie it on when he found that it was blunt in the hook, or unsatisfactory in some way now forgotten. He replaced it, and took instead a teal and green, a fly exactly similar except that it had a green body instead of a red one. I asked him why he had changed the fly. He said he had not changed, and after some talk at cross-purposes it emerged that he did not see any difference. The green and the red looked alike to him. He had not previously known that he was colour-blind.

This explained a point that had puzzled me, for he had often matched flies that did not appear to me to be similar. It is also, perhaps, the explanation of his being so good at catching trout. Perhaps red and green, as normal people see them, look alike to trout, so that the artificial flies that looked to him exactly like the natural flies looked like natural flies to the trout also, which therefore rose to them. This explanation has at least the merit of consoling less successful fishermen.

So here we have a genuine puzzle. You and I go about the world assuming that when we are seeing or knowing red things and green things we are seeing or knowing things that are really different. No doubt you had not thought of saying this explicitly, but you do make that assumption. He, on the other hand, was going about the world on the assumption that red and green, as we call them, are not different. This is a very elementary and limited example, but it does show that knowing even anything so apparently simple as a green trout fly and a red one must be extremely complicated ; and it does show also that different people can have different assumptions about knowing.

The assumptions that we all make to begin with about knowing and explaining and so forth are, as we shall go on to see, very muddled and unsatisfactory. This is a very serious practical handicap, because in many cases a problem is difficult for us to solve, not because of the difficulty of the problem itself, but because there is something unsatisfactory in our assumptions about the nature of knowing. There are many difficulties in science, in economics, in politics, and in the understanding of the affairs of daily life, which are not due to the difficulties of the subjects themselves, but are due to the muddled and unsatisfactory assumptions we have made, unawares, about the nature of knowing.

CHAPTER III

The Traditional Explanation of Perception I.

W E all go about our daily lives on the assumption that differently coloured things are really differently coloured. If we did not assume this, we should behave differently. Unless we assumed that the red light on the traffic signal at the cross-roads was really red and really different from the green light, we should not be able to rely on one of them as indicating that it was legal for us to cross the road, and on the other as indicating that it was illegal and unsafe for us to do so. This can be put in another way by saying that we must already have assumed that the lights exist and that they are what they are, whatever you or I may think about them. In other words, we have assumed that the objects around us exist independently of us. This is what we all think, to begin with at least.

This seems clear enough, and yet there is a difficulty. You and I and the policeman (assuming that you are not red/green colour-blind) can all tell the red light from the green one without any trouble, and so we think no more about it. But there are people, like my friend of student days, who cannot see any difference between two patches of colour, say red and green, which to you and me are conspicuously different. You may perhaps have among your acquaintances someone who has difficulty in distinguishing a green traffic light at a crossing from a red one, and who therefore always looks to see whether the light in question is the uppermost or the lowermost on the traffic-light standard, because he knows that the red or ' stop ' light is at the top, and the green or ' go ' light is at the bottom. If, as on a dark and foggy night, he cannot see the standard but only the light itself, he may be quite incapable of saying whether the light indicates 'stop' or 'go'.

The number of such people is very small in proportion to the population as a whole, and very much smaller among women than among men. But we are not entitled to disregard such people, merely because they are few and we are in the majority, and to dismiss them airily on the ground that they must have something wrong with them. This will not do. The colour-blind people could equally say that there is something wrong with us, because we see two patches of colour as being different, when they are really the same. This kind of dispute leads nowhere.

The point is that some people can look at what I am looking at, and yet what they see is different from what I see. They see only one colour. I see two definitely different colours. So it now seems that there must be something wrong with the assumption we have been making all these years without noticing it. There seems to be something wrong with the assumption that differently coloured things are really differently coloured, and that they exist independently of us. It now begins to look as if the objects around us did *not* exist independently of us. There is clearly something wrong somewhere in the assumptions we have all unthinkingly made as to the existence by themselves of the familiar objects around us. What can we do about it ?

This is where we must turn for help to the philosophers. In ancient and medieval times many attempts had been made by them to explain these and similar puzzling facts. No one explanation, however, had ever been generally accepted until a theory called the 'representative' theory of perception was formulated in the seventeenth century, the period which is usually reckoned as the beginning time of modern philosophy. This theory is in fact very much older and can be found in the writings of Saint Augustine in the fifth century, but it is known to-day mainly in the form given to it in the seventeenth century by Descartes and John Locke.[1] Many other thinkers, including Galileo who was a slightly older contemporary of Descartes, contributed to the working out in detail of the theory, but it was Descartes' work that made it widely known. It then came to be almost universally held by philosophers, in one form or another, and it has passed into such common acceptance beyond philosophical circles that it is often assumed by people who have never given a thought to Descartes or to any philosopher. It became the traditional explanation of the puzzling facts of sense perception.

We shall later find that there is something profoundly wrong with this theory. However, we must understand it before we can hope to advance to something better. Understanding the theory of representative perception is therefore our immediate task. It gives a straightforward and sensible explanation, so far as it goes, and you will probably find, as you read of it in Descartes or Locke or in the simplified exposition here, that you are coming to accept it, or at least to be much influenced by it. This is an instance of the way in which our individual philosophical development runs rapidly through the same main

---

[1] René Descartes (1596–1650). Brought up in a Jesuit College in France, but expounded his characteristic doctrines (Cartesianism) ostensibly as an alternative to the medieval philosophy of the scholastics, though he was still in fact profoundly influenced by them. His representationism was published in his *Discourse on Method* and in his *Meditations*. Was also a distinguished mathematician, and invented analytical geometry.

John Locke (1632–1704). A doctor of medicine, an F.R.S., and at one time an Under-Secretary of State in the Government of William III after the Revolution of 1689. Wrote a small book on education with a modern tang to it. His philosophical views were published in his *Essay Concerning Human Understanding*.

successive stages as did the development of the generations of our predecessors.

What Descartes and Locke said about the way in which we perceive the material objects around us was in effect as follows. Here I am, and I see things and shapes and colours ; I feel hot things and cold things ; I feel pains and I feel pleasures ; I smell smells ; and so forth. These all seem quite real. They do not feel like illusions. They are not illusions. You can put your fingers round this book which you are now reading, and feel it. It is not an illusion that you are holding, but a quite real, material book. And yet, those experiences of colour-blind persons make it appear that there must be something wrong with this assumption that what I see and hear and touch and feel really exists, because somebody else sees not what I see, but something different.

What I see and hear and feel, said Descartes and Locke and other philosophers, may very well exist for me (whatever precisely that may mean) ; and what some other man sees and hears and feels may very well exist for him. Perhaps, they suggested, what I am seeing is one thing, and what he is seeing is some other thing, no doubt largely similar but not the same thing. This would explain why the red and green traffic lights looked different to me while to him they looked the same, for on this theory I have a picture or representation in my mind of the cross-roads with the traffic lights, and in my representation of it the lights shining to stop the cross traffic are different in colour from the lights shining to let the main-road traffic pass ; while the other man has his picture or representation in his mind, and in his representation the lights are more or less the same and very difficult or impossible to distinguish.

This, said the philosophers who suggested it, must be the reason why each of us is so convinced that what he sees is real, even though what he sees is not the same as what somebody else sees in apparently the same situation. On this theory, what each man sees is a picture or representation inside his mind of the real public situation outside his mind. It is entirely real to him, and he sees it very clearly. This cannot be denied. We cannot assert that the colour-blind man does not in fact see the two lights as the same colour. He will make a very definite comment if we do. On this theory which is associated with the names of Descartes and Locke, these difficulties we have encountered cease to be puzzling. On their theory, each of us has his own picture in his own mind. What I see is not the external real world, but is only a picture or representation of it formed inside my mind. What you see is similarly not the external real world, but is only a picture or representation of it formed inside your mind ; and what the colour-blind man sees is not the external real world, but only a picture or representation of it formed inside his mind. It happens that you and I have very similar pictures, while the colour-blind man has one that is different in some respects.

So, according to this theory, it turns out in the end not to be surprising that different people see things differently, or to speak more exactly, that different people have different pictures or representations in their minds. I have my picture in my mind, and you have yours in your mind. It is in fact rather the opposite of surprising that these different pictures should be a little different.

Moreover, say Descartes and Locke and those who think like them, consider what sort of sensory organs we have, what sort of eyes and ears and fingers we have to see and hear and feel with. If you do this, say those philosophers, you can understand how each of us builds up his own picture in his own mind, and how it is impossible for him to do anything else.

Think of your eye. Our natural first notion about our eyes is that an eye is a kind of window we look out of. It is not. It is not a sort of peep-hole in your head through which you survey the world. On the contrary, it is a hole in your head which lets light-rays in. In front of it, in the pupil, there is a lens, much like the lens of a camera. There is an iris too, which functions like the variable stop in a camera, to allow in more light on a dull day and less on a sunny day by enlarging or contracting a hole in front of the middle of the lens. When light-rays from the sun or from some other source of illumination fall on objects round about us they are reflected, i.e. they bounce off, and some of them fall on the lens of the eye. The lens focuses these light-rays, i.e. it bends them into tidy little cone-shaped groups and directs them neatly on to the retina, which is the small surface about the size of a sixpence on the inside of the back of the eyeball. This retina is sensitive to light in much the same way as a camera film, so that when light falls on it, certain chemical and other changes take place in it. When these changes take place in the retina, in consequence of its having light-rays falling upon it, then the nerves in it are affected and nervous impulses, as they are called, start to move along the nerves from the eye to the brain. These nerves, incidentally, do not go from the eye to the front of the brain as one might expect, but to the back of the brain. Then, after the nervous impulses have finally reached the brain, and only then, we have the experience we call ' seeing '. ' Seeing ' is not by any means as direct and simple as we commonly think.

At this moment you are looking at this page. You see it and the print on it. Consider what is happening. Light-rays travelling quite astonishingly fast are coming from the sun or from the lamp in your room. Some of those rays are falling on the page, and of those that do fall on the page, some are being absorbed and some are being bounced off. Of these latter, some are falling on the pupil of your eye. Others—different ones—may be falling on the pupils of the eyes of any other people who may happen to be in the room with you. Those that fall on your eyes are passing through the pupil and the lens and are being bent in passing through. (If you wear glasses they will have been bent already before reaching your eye.) These light-rays go through the clear jelly that fills the middle of your eye, and then they reach the back of your eyeball, where they touch the retina.

Now very remarkable things start happening. Complicated chemical and other changes take place in your retina, and then more changes in the nerve, or rather bundle of nerves like a telephone cable, which connects your eye with the back of your brain. Try tracing with your finger the path they follow. Put your finger above your cheekbone behind your eye and draw it straight back, just above the top of your ear. That is roughly the line along which these nervous impulses are passing. Move your finger further back until it is very near the back of your head. Now move it up a little. This brings your finger very near to the point where the nervous impulses enter the brain itself. These 'nervous impulses' move along that nerve surprisingly slowly. They are very far from instantaneous. A fighter aircraft travels much faster. When those nervous impulses which started in your retina at the back of your eyeball have at last reached your brain, then in some way we do not in the least understand, you have the experience that we refer to as 'seeing the page'. You do not have that experience until the lengthy and complicated processes here roughly outlined have been completed.

So our old simple assumption that things exist 'out there', and that we simply see them directly as they are, seems to be contrary to the facts. Many queer and complicated happenings have to take place before we can have the experience we call ' seeing '. Further, did you notice, in passing, one curiously thought-provoking point ? Owing to the time-lag in the passing of the nervous impulse from your eye to your brain, you are not seeing what is affecting your eye *now*, because the nervous impulse starting in your retina *now* has not yet reached your brain. What you are seeing *now* is what affected your eye a short time ago, a fraction of a second ago. That is to say, we never see, and never can see, the present. All we can ever see is the recent past. It is the very recent past but, however recent, it is definitely the past. When we see it, it has already ceased to exist.

These and many other points that emerge from an examination of our sensory organs would be understandable if, as some philosophers say, we are not seeing the page itself (or whatever example we take) but are seeing instead only the private picture or representation that each of us has in his mind, composed of the sensations produced by those nervous impulses which follow that devious pathway and end in the backs of our brains.

Further, this view of these philosophers can explain a point that has probably already disturbed any reader who is interested in modern developments in physics. The physicists say that the table I am writing on, and the chair you are sitting in, may seem to be solid and at rest and yet are not in fact solid at all. They consist, say the physicists, of electrons, protons, neutrons and so forth, immensely far apart relative to their own size, whirling about at immense speeds. The apparently solid table top is mostly vacant space with numbers of minute entities occupying it, much as a small armed force occupies a large area by moving rapidly all over it ceaselessly.

If tables and chairs and books and traffic lights

and trout flies really do consist of minute moving entities immensely far apart, rushing hither and thither in a largely vacant space, it requires to be explained how our ordinary experience of them is so different. The theory of Descartes and Locke would explain this, for on their view the light-rays bounced off by those entities fall on our eyes and cause those various and complicated nervous processes which end in the brain, and thus in some unknown way cause sensations in our minds, and those sensations go to build up our own private pictures or representations of the table or book or whatever it is, these representations being naturally not in the least like the particles of which the table or book is really composed. On this theory it is not surprising that the representation created in your mind, and the representation created in my mind, and the representation created in the mind of a man who is colour-blind, should be all somewhat different one from another. And yet your representation is perfectly real to you; it is in your mind. My representation is perfectly real to me; it is in my mind. And the colour-blind man's representation is perfectly real to him; it is in his mind.

The same conclusions emerge from an examination of the experience we call 'hearing'. Similar processes occur, except that it is air-waves and not light-waves that fall on the organ in question. Air is an extremely elastic substance, and when any object in contact with air vibrates for any reason, little waves of alternately high and low pressure in the air surrounding it are sent spreading out in all directions. These are reflected almost unchanged by hard smooth surfaces, and are largely absorbed by soft and irregular ones, which is why we hear a strong echo to our footsteps if we walk through a large unfurnished room, and hear no echo in a room containing furniture and hangings. Some of those air-waves fall on the ears of any listening human being or animal. These alternate waves of high and low air-pressure pass down the hole in the side of the head called the ear and press upon the ear drum, which is a thin skin stretched across the hole like a drum-head, and they make it vibrate to their own rate of vibration. On the inner side of this drum is an arrangement of three small levers of bone which transmit the movement to another piece of thin skin stretched across another hole still further inside the bone of the skull. This hole is filled with liquid, which in consequence vibrates in time to the original air-waves. Inside this liquid is a narrow little bag, curled round like a snail shell, filled with still another liquid, which similarly vibrates in time to the original air-waves. Little nerve-endings like hairs project inside this bag into the inner liquid, so that when it moves to and fro these nerve-endings are bent, which causes nervous impulses to start in them. These impulses pass along the bundle of nerves leading to the brain. Then, when the nervous impulses have at last reached the brain, we have the experience we call 'hearing a sound'. Here again there is a slight time-lag in the passage of the nervous impulse, so, strictly speaking, we never can hear what anyone is *saying* to us, but only what he has just said a fraction of a second before.

The same sort of situation is occurring in the working of all our other sense-organs also. Our sensations of touch, for instance, come from little nerve-endings just under the surface of the skin. If you put the forefinger of your right hand on this book, and have the sensation of touching it, then what is happening is that the nerve-endings just under the surface of the skin are being stimulated by the contact, and are emitting nervous impulses which travel along a nerve which passes up your finger, up your arm, across your shoulder and into the middle of your spine, and up inside your skull, into your brain. Then, when the impulses have at last reached your brain, and not before, you have, in some way we do not understand, the sensation of touching the book with your forefinger.

Descartes and Locke could make out a very convincing case for their view that what we experience are not real things themselves, but only representations of them formed in our minds out of the many different sensations that are caused to arise in our minds in those very complicated and roundabout ways. Descartes and Locke did not of course mean that we are conscious of the different constituents as separate sensations and that we then consciously and deliberately construct the total picture out of them by fitting them together, as we could build a house by consciously and deliberately fitting together its constituent bricks and timber. What we are conscious of, they said, is the finished representation in our minds. It is only by special inquiry that we discover how that finished representation or picture in our minds came to be made up into what it is.

We may subsequently find out that there is something altogether wrong with this theory of theirs, but at this stage it seems sensible, and indeed it appears inevitable as an explanation when once it has been pointed out.

I hope the reader can now see from experience what I meant when saying in the first chapter that something would happen to him when he started studying philosophy. After thinking along with Descartes and Locke, as we have been doing here in a small way, we no longer go on assuming, as we used unthinkingly to do, that the things round us are simply there as we see them. When we realize what appears to be happening in the processes of seeing and hearing and in experiencing by the other sense-organs, we realize that we are not directly knowing things as they are. It appears that what each of us is knowing directly is the representation inside his mind composed of the sensations produced by the workings of the eyes and ears and other sense-organs.

This brings us to a somewhat strange and unexpected position. Instead of thinking, as we used to do, that we all see and hear and experience a public real world, we have been brought to think that we do not experience the real world at all. We seem to be totally and permanently cut off from it. We never experience it, and never can. Instead, what we each experience is a kind of mental picture. What I experience is my mental picture, and that is all. What you experience is your mental picture, and that is all. And what the next man experiences is his mental picture, and that is all. Each of us, according to this theory, is shut up inside his own mind. This is the point to which our inquiries have now brought us.

The puzzle then is no longer that different people have somewhat different experiences of the same situation. The puzzle now is that different people should have experiences that are even approximately the same, as apparently they are, for we can get through life tolerably well together and can understand each other at least for most practical purposes. This puzzle is however not so serious as it at first appears, and Descartes and Locke were able to give a quite good explanation of why our experiences should be similar in some respects and different in others, and to this we shall now go on.

CHAPTER IV

The Traditional Explanation of Perception II.

THIS theory deserves a second chapter to itself, for it seems at first excessively novel and strange even to those who have already come across applications of it, as many have, for instance in laboratory work in the sciences. It is perhaps simpler to understand as applied to memory.

Suppose that a man is asked to describe some small place in which he had been vividly happy long ago, but had not visited since. He could of course remember it, and he could give quite a good description of it. Yet we all know from previous similar experiences of our own that if he were to visit it again, he would be surprised to find that much of it was very different from what he remembered it as being. He would find that he had altogether forgotten some parts, and that he had remembered some other parts of it in the wrong relation to one another. He would probably say, somewhat wistfully, 'How different it is from what I've been thinking it was all those years.' He might even say: 'How different it is from the picture of it I've been carrying about in my mind's eye all those years.'

He could not say this unless he had assumed, of course without necessarily being articulately aware of it, the theory that when we remember a situation in the past we are not seeing that past situation itself directly, but are seeing only a memory-picture of it which is present in our minds now. On this view we explain inaccuracies and gaps in memory by saying that the memory-picture is incomplete or distorted, as we say of a bad portrait that it is a bad portrait because it does not resemble the person whom it is meant to resemble. We tend to take this view of memory quite naturally. That is to say, we have presupposed the representative view of knowledge as far as memory, i.e. knowledge of the past, is concerned. (This is, incidentally, a striking instance of the way in which we can hold an assumption even about a matter as abstruse and philosophic as the nature of memory-knowledge without realizing that we hold it.)

The representationist philosophers argued in effect that this seems a very sound and very reasonable account of knowledge as far as knowledge of the past is concerned, and that knowledge of the present will probably turn out, on further inquiry, to be of the same kind.

Notice, too, that just as we assume the representative theory of knowledge about knowledge of the past, so in certain cases do we already assume it about knowledge of the present also. If somebody says : ' I'm sure there is a plane flying around up there ', and if nobody else can see or hear any plane, then that person will say : ' That's odd. I certainly heard the sound of a plane's engines. It must just have been an idea.' He means that the idea of the sound of an aircraft's engines existed genuinely in his mind or consciousness, even though there was not in fact any aircraft in the external public world corresponding to the idea in his mind.

In certain cases, then, it appears that we presuppose the representative theory of knowledge where knowledge of the present is concerned, but in certain cases only, for we assuredly do not presuppose it in all cases. This is a humbling example of the way in which we sometimes go on one presupposition and sometimes on a different and contradictory one, without being aware of our own inconsistency.

This representative theory of knowledge, which in a vague and muddled way we already tend to presuppose in some cases, and which we become more inclined to adopt fully and consistently on becoming familiar with it as explicitly stated by Descartes and

Locke, has many advantages. It gives for instance a quite good explanation of the difference between truth and error. It gives an explanation of the difference between true knowledge and illusion. If the picture or representation in my mind, which is all that I can ever know, is like the real things in the outer world, which I can never know, then, we say, I have true knowledge. If, on the other hand, the mental picture does not correspond accurately to the real things, then we say that we are suffering an illusion or have made a mistake, and that this alleged knowledge is not a genuine representation of what exists.

In the light of all this, let us return for a moment to our colour-blind man and his traffic lights, and the difficulty which his existence raised for us. How is it that he can see only one colour where other men can see two? We can explain this on the representative theory of knowledge. On this theory, there exists out in the real world something very mysterious. The physicists say that it consists of rushing particles very far apart relative to their own minute size. Whatever it is, it is the outer real world, and according to the representative theory we cannot directly experience it. Instead, according to the theory, I have inside my mind a picture or representation of the cross-roads with their traffic lights. In it, the lights shining in one direction are a different colour from those shining in the cross direction. At the same time the colour-blind man has his representation in his mind, and in his representation the lights are the same colour, while in the real world there are not any colours at all. In the real world there are only those swarms of tiny particles swirling about at enormous velocities, or electro-magnetic vibrations rippling along through space. The real world has not got any colour. This of course does not mean that the real world is some neutral grey, or some vague colour. It means that the real world is such that it does not have any colour. It cannot have colour. Only the pictures in my mind, and the pictures in your mind, can have colours. The real world, on this theory, is such that it causes sensations of colour to arise in our minds, through the complicated and devious working of the sensory organs and brain, but in itself has no colour. We *think* the real world has colours, but these colours are only colour sensations in our minds, and when we impute them to the real world, as we do in our unenlightened days, we are making a mistake.

So the colour-blind man is not wrong when he says that the two lights are the same colour; and we are not wrong when we say that they are different colours. Neither he nor we on this theory can be either right or wrong. Each of us, when he says and believes he sees a patch of colour in the external world, is according to this theory seeing only the private picture or colour-sensation in his own mind. Consequently if you say that you see one colour and I say that I see another, we are not contradicting each other, because we are talking about different things. You are talking about your private picture or representation, and I am talking about mine.

On this theory, the situation is as it would be if we were discussing pains. If you and I both had headaches, and I said : ' The pain is a shooting, sharp pain ', and you said : ' The pain is a steady, dull one ', then neither you nor I nor anybody else would think that we were contradicting each other. I am talking about *my* pain, and you are talking about *your* pain. On this theory, colours are only sensations in my mind, as a pain is admittedly only a sensation in my mind. Further—and this is a point of some importance to which we shall return later— a colour exists only so long as I am conscious of it, precisely as a pain exists only so long as I am conscious of it, and for the same reason, namely that there is no external real colour common to us all, any more than there is any external real pain common to us all. There exist only my pain and your pain, my colour and your colour; and, just as a pain exists only as long as I experience it, so, on this theory, does a colour exist only so long as I experience it.

Other qualities like colour, such as warmth and cold, smell, and sound and taste, turn out similarly, according to the representative theory, to be no more than sensations in my mind, existing in my mind only so long as I am aware of them, and not existing at all in the real world. The warmth I feel, and the sound I hear, may in some mysterious way be similar to the warmth you feel at the same time and the sound you hear at the same time, but mine are in my mind, and yours are in your mind. They are none of them in the external world at all.

This leads us to view the world as being really one in which there is no colour, no sound, no warmth, no cold, no smell, no taste. On this theory, all these are private sensations like pains. If anyone were to assert that there were real aches and pains in the external world, and that they were not merely sensations in our minds, then clearly he would be under an illusion. According to Locke and Descartes we are all in fact under precisely the same sort of illusion when we think that colours and sounds and tastes and smells and warmth and cold exist in the real world. According to them, only the study of philosophy, meaning thereby the acceptance of their theories, can emancipate us from this illusion.

You will probably feel that there must be something wrong here, for it surely cannot be the case that all qualities are unreal, and exist only as sensations in our minds, even though we may for the moment grant to Descartes and Locke that some are. These philosophers provided for this. Their argument continued as follows.

Suppose that I lay down a pencil on the folding table on which I am writing, and that you look at it and see that its colour is, say, yellow. Let us suppose that it is a new pencil, so that the paint on it is vivid and uniform. If I were to say that its colour was not yellow, but was in fact green like the canvas top of the table, then you would probably shrug your shoulders and say, in view of our recent discussion : 'Well, I suppose the sensations of colour he gets in his consciousness from the pencil and from the table top are similar, though the sensations I get in my consciousness are very different.' You would probably add : 'We must leave it at that. He and I just have different sensations. The real pencil is neither yellow nor green. It consists only of those minute and mysterious particles that the physicists talk of, and it hasn't got any colour.' This appears reasonable.

But suppose I make a statement of a different kind. Suppose I say : 'The pencil is the same length as the matchbox lying beside it.' This time you do not say : 'Well, I suppose he sees it like that.' This time you say : 'That was all very well about colours. I can quite understand how different people could have different sensations of colour in their minds, but I just do not believe that anybody looking at that six-inch-long pencil and that two-inch-long matchbox could possibly get the sensation that they are the same length.' I should then have to admit that in fact I do not see pencil and matchbox as the same length. The one looks about three times the length of the other.

This brings out a notable point. According to this theory of Descartes and Locke, I have my own private sensations where colour, or warmth, or sound is concerned, and these may or may not resemble your similarly private ones. But where length is concerned, the state of affairs seems to be different. You may be willing to believe that I see the colour of the pencil differently from you, but you just do not believe that I can see a new pencil and a matchbox as the same length. And of course I do not in fact see them as the same length.

From this, it begins to look as if things had two different kinds of qualities, namely qualities like colour and qualities like length. Examples of qualities like colour, as we realize if we think it over, are sound, heat (and cold), taste, smell, and touch (smooth, rough, silky, etc.). Examples of qualities like length are number and motion.

If I take five pennies from my pocket and throw them on the table, and if you and I compare notes as to the qualities which we think that these pennies possess, then we should find the following. About the number of them, we should not disagree. If I were to say that I saw six when you saw five, you would not believe me—unless of course there were some temporary optical illusion of some kind—and as a matter of fact I should see only five. That is to say we could not disagree about the number of them. About the motion of them too we could not disagree. If you saw one still rolling on its edge in ever-decreasing circles, and I said that I saw them all lying motionless, again you would not believe me, and again I should have to admit that I did in fact see them as you did.

But if you said that the coins were cold, and I said that they were warm, you would be willing to agree that each of us might be having his private and different sensations. I might have come in out of a cold and wet night, in contrast to which the coins gave me a sensation of mild warmth. You might have been sitting beside the fire and have become so thoroughly warm that the coins gave you a sensation of cold when you touched them. There is a traditional trick which you can try upon yourself to illustrate this point in your own sensations. Run very cold water on your left hand and very hot water on your right hand. Then place both hands in a basin of tepid water. You will have from the same water a sensation of heat in the left hand and of cold in the right hand.

The same holds of smell and taste, and is indeed notorious of them. It holds also of sound. If you are on one train going north and I am on another train going south, and if we pass each other at speed and my train blows its whistle, then as we approach each other you will hear the note of that whistle at a certain pitch, but after we have passed you will hear it as a lower pitch as my train recedes behind you. At the same time the pitch of the whistle will not vary to me, but will remain the same. I have my sensation of sound in my mind; you have yours in your mind. It is not surprising that we should disagree about the pitch of the note. As to the motion of the trains on the other hand we could not disagree. It would not be possible for me to have the experience that they were stationary beside each other, while you had the experience that they were passing at speed. Sound, like heat, seems to be one kind of quality, while motion is a different kind of quality.

Locke gave names to these two kinds. He called the qualities such as length and motion the *primary* qualities, because the object really possesses them. They are real. They are primary. And he called the other qualities, such as colour, sound, warmth and taste, the *secondary* qualities, because the object does not really possess them. They are not real. They are only secondary. They exist not in the real world, but only in the private world that each one of us pictures in his own mind.

This theory seems odd at first acquaintance, but when we think it over, it comes to appear quite sensible. In particular it explains certain complex procedures which we all adopt without troubling to consider why we adopt them. Both in scientific inquiry and in the common affairs of daily life we are repeatedly making efforts to obtain observations about which different observers will not disagree, and on which appropriate action can reliably be taken. Consider what a doctor does when he takes a patient's temperature. He does not put his finger in the patient's mouth, or under his armpit, and then announce that he is ' running a temperature ' or is ' normal '. A doctor does not do this, for the very sound reason that his judgement would vary according to his own bodily condition at the moment. Further, if he relied only on his own feeling, he would have no means of convincing another doctor who assessed the patient's temperature differently, nor of convincing the patient himself. The doctor uses a clinical thermometer instead, and when he reads his thermometer everybody concerned accepts that reading, whatever he may feel.

What is happening here, according to Descartes and Locke, is as follows. The patient's body, on their theory, has the primary qualities of size and motion, as have the particles of which it is composed ; and the rate of vibration of these particles constitutes the heat of the body (meaning of course, ' heat ' as dealt with by the physicists, not ' heat ' as the feeling of warmth, which is a secondary quality private to the mind of each separate observer). A man may feel warm, but this only means that the representation of his body that he has in his own mind has the secondary quality of warmth. His body in itself is just as much an affair of gyrating particles as is the table or the desk. It has not got the secondary quality of warmth any more than they have.

The representation of the patient's body which the doctor holds in his mind has the quality of warmth, just as the representation that some other doctor holds in his mind has warmth, and just as the representation of his body that the patient himself holds in his own mind has warmth ; but his representation may not be like the patient's, nor like the other doctor's, and so they may disagree.

When, however, a doctor uses a thermometer, he is no longer relying on a feeling, but on the length of a thread of mercury. This length is a primary quality, and hence all agree about it. The length of the thread of mercury varies according to the temperature of any object with which it is brought into heat-conducting proximity. In using a thermometer we are therefore replacing a judgement about a secondary quality, which is private to each observer, by a judgement about a primary quality, which is objective and independent of the observer, so that the representation of it in one man's mind is the same as the representation of it in another man's mind.

In the same way, disagreement about sound, which is a secondary quality, can be settled by reference to some primary quality which varies in keeping with the secondary quality. For instance, I may try to tune a piano wire to middle C, and you may maintain that I have tuned it flat. We could argue endlessly about this without ever finding a common standard, because musical notes are secondary qualities, so that I have mine in my mind and you have your possibly different ones in yours. There is, on this theory, no real musical note in the external world. In the external world, however, there really is a piano wire of a definite length, vibrating a definite number of times per second. So we fetch a middle C tuning fork, so made that it vibrates 261 times a second, and we stretch or slacken the piano wire until it vibrates at exactly the same number of times a second, as can be measured by a smoke-drum or similar apparatus. When that is done we all agree, because we are dealing with primary qualities which are real, and not with secondary qualities which are merely private representations existing in our minds and nowhere else.

If you have worked through the argument up to this point, you will have an understanding of the essential points in the traditional theory of representative perception, and may adopt it, though with some misgivings, in explaining your own experiences as you look about you.

The representative theory of perception stated here is of course only one element in the more complete theories of knowledge propounded by Descartes and Locke and others. It applies only to the perception of material objects around us. (To account for mathematical knowledge, for instance, Descartes had an additional and different theory.) As we shall see later, underlying this more limited theory about our experience of material objects there is a question of very much wider importance as to the nature of knowing in general, and to this wider issue we shall return at an appropriate point. In the meantime we shall restrict ourselves to the narrower theory as here stated, and to certain very remarkable developments which arise out of it.

Our present position is that we have come to an understanding of the representationist theory of perception by a series of steps which appear reasonable, so much so that it seems likely that if Descartes and Locke had not developed it, then somebody else sooner or later would have done so. But we cannot stop here. There is a curious and disturbing consequence of the representative theory of perception to which we find ourselves driven if we are serious in our inquiry. This was pointed out in a conspicuous way by a very remarkable Irishman, George Berkeley,[1] at the beginning of the eighteenth century. By doing so he caused bewilderment and exasperation to his contemporaries, and he has done the same to each successive generation of his new readers ever since.

[1] George Berkeley (1684–1753). Wrote an essay on *A New Theory of Vision* while at Trinity College, Dublin. Published his 'Berkeleian Idealism' in his *Principles of Human Knowledge* while still a young man. Spent some years in a quixotic missionary enterprise in the West Indies and Rhode Island. Later became Bishop of Cloyne in the south of Ireland.

CHAPTER V

Bishop Berkeley's Deductions

BISHOP BERKELEY is a much misunderstood person. Most of us have probably heard of him only as an eccentric Irish philosopher who maintained that sticks and stones and all material things are 'merely imaginary'. This is a parody of what he said, but it is admittedly a not altogether surprising misunderstanding, for what he had to say did at first hearing sound as if that was what he intended. He did not of course mean anything so absurd and unreasonable. Indeed, when we find out what he did say, it appears so inevitable a deduction from the representationist theory of perception that we may well believe that if Berkeley had not drawn it, then somebody else would have done so at some time sooner or later.

This does not mean that we come to agree with the views that Berkeley held. It only means that we come to see that if anybody starts thinking, as the representationist philosophers did, about the way in which we perceive material objects around us, then if he is remorselessly logical, he will in the end find himself thinking like Berkeley, whether he likes it or not.

Let us recapitulate the position we have reached, and take stock of it. When we consider pains and pleasures and experiences of such kinds, we are all agreed on certain points. We are all agreed that pains exist in the consciousness of the man who feels them, and nowhere else. In other words, there are no real pains existing by themselves in the external world independently of whether anybody feels them or not. The *causes* of the pains may, we say, be common to us all, as for instance if you and I both get burned by the same fire, but the pains are private. I have in my consciousness my pain, which undoubtedly exists as long as I feel it, and you have yours in your consciousness. We may happen to have similar pains at the same time, as for instance if we both develop toothache at the same time, but it would never occur to anybody to explain this by saying that there existed in the external world some one real toothache which both of us were experiencing at the same time. That would be patently absurd. Each has his own private pain, and that private pain exists only as long as he is feeling it. Pains and such sensations are ' mind-dependent '. ' Existing ', as far as pains are concerned, means ' being experienced '.

Now, according to the theory outlined in the preceding chapter, colours and all the secondary qualities are ' mind-dependent ' also, and for the same reasons. If the colour green, which I in my unsophisticated moments think is in the canvas top of my table, does not really exist in the canvas at all (as the theory says) but only exists in my mental representation of the table, then that colour green is ' mind-dependent ' and exists only so long as I am conscious of it, just as the colour that you in your unsophisticated moments think exists in the canvas really exists only in your mental representation of the table, and likewise exists only so long as you are conscious of it.

Consider further what this involves. By going on step by step in this way, with the aid of Descartes and Locke, we have been brought to the conclusion that the secondary qualities of objects do not exist independently of us in the real world. (Again, bear in mind that this is a conclusion to which we are brought only if we start as Descartes and Locke did, and follow them. We may later find out that there is something wrong with the way in which they started.) To put it more exactly, the tables and chairs and all else that I see and hear, are as I experience them only a picture or representation caused to arise in my mind by a complicated succession of happenings in my eyes and ears and other sense-organs and in my nerves and brain ; and a very large proportion of that picture or representation, namely all the secondary qualities, has nothing whatever corresponding to it in the outer real world. Only the primary qualities in the representation have any counterparts in the external real world.

So it looks as if our daily experience were an enormous illusion. The world that each of us experiences (more exactly, the representations that we each of us have in our own minds) is an illusion. It is not an adequate copy of the real world, because so many of the more interesting and enjoyable parts of it, the colours and scents and so forth, do not exist in the real world. The real world is colourless, soundless, and altogether without any of the secondary qualities. Moreover, all those colours and scents and so forth that I experience exist in my mind only as long as I am conscious of them, while the colours and scents that you experience (different colours and different scents from mine) similarly exist in your mind only so long as you are conscious of them.

If our experience really is an illusion (I expect you will say), then it is a convenient and desirable illusion, for if we were to see things as they really are, the world would be regrettably dull. If we experienced things as they really are (that is, as on the representative theory of perception they really are) then if we went for a walk in the country on a spring morning, we should presumably experience only those gyrating, soundless, colourless particles which the physicists tell us about, i.e. the primary qualities only, and we should experience none of the interesting and enjoyable secondary qualities. There would be no blue in the sky, no white in the clouds, no bird song, no scent in the woodlands, no sound of

water splashing over the stones, because all these are
secondary qualities, and therefore do not exist in the
real world. They are added in some way to the
representation which each of us has in his own mind.

This is, very roughly outlined, the account that
Descartes and Locke and many other philosophers
gave of the world we live in and of our knowledge of
it. This view is still held and taught to-day by many
scientists who have not come in contact with later
developments in philosophy. At the beginning of
the eighteenth century the gist of it was held by all
philosophers.

Let me impress upon the reader once again that
this view is a view that one comes to hold if one
starts this inquiry as Descartes and Locke did, but
not necessarily otherwise. We of the last three
hundred years do in fact all start philosophizing
much as they did, i.e. we start with the same unrecognized presuppositions about the nature of
knowledge, and hence this view of theirs which I have
been outlining (the primary qualities as alone real, the
secondary qualities as private and mind-dependent,
etc.) appears to us to be on the whole true, when
once it is explained to us. Most of us to-day are in
very much the same position, as far as our views and
assumptions about the nature of knowledge are concerned, as were the professional philosophers at the
beginning of the eighteenth century.

At this point Berkeley appeared. He constituted
a disquieting incursion upon the calm of the philosophers and others who tried to understand him, for he
told them, in effect, that Locke's views were all very
well as far as they went, but that it was illogical to
stop where he stopped. There was, he said, a further
step which had to be taken, and this further step was
a very disturbing one.

His line of argument ran as follows. We are all
agreed that pains do not exist independently. There

are no pains existing as real entities in the world whether anybody experiences them or not. Pains are 'mind-dependent'. This is agreed about pains, and, says Berkeley, it is also agreed about colours and all the secondary qualities. But now, what about the primary qualities? Berkeley says that they, too, are mind-dependent. The primary qualities of the pencil and the matchbox are, he maintains, mind-dependent in precisely the same way as the colour of the pencil and the pain from a burned finger.

This is Bishop Berkeley's conclusion, and at first sight it is undeniably astonishing. It means that I have in my mind my picture or representation, primary and secondary qualities and all; and you have in your mind your picture, primary and secondary qualities and all; and the next man has in his mind his picture, primary and secondary qualities and all. Each man's picture exists for him alone and only so long as he is conscious of it. And that, says Berkeley, is all that exists. Apart from me (my mind or self, not my body) and my picture in my mind, and you and your picture, and the next man and his picture, and so on, there is not anything. There is, he says, no independently existing real world at all.

If this assertion of Berkeley's were made to you without any historical introduction, it would appear fantastic and absurd, but when you understand the representationist theory which was part of the intellectual atmosphere in which Berkeley grew up, you can see not only how he came quite naturally to his conclusion by taking the next step, but also how logically he *had* to come to that conclusion. You may or may not agree with Berkeley's conclusion itself. The point is that if you accept the theory of perception that we have been discussing up to this stage, then Berkeley's next step follows quite naturally, and is indeed inevitable.

This argument is at first somewhat elusive, so

it may be as well to run over it again in slightly different terms. The fundamental point in the representative theory of perception is that we do not experience objects directly. All that we can ever know is a private world of experience in our own minds. We have seen on further inquiry that some parts of that experience have nothing corresponding to them in the outer world, namely pains and pleasures and the like. We have also seen that other parts, namely the secondary qualities, have similarly nothing corresponding to them in the outer world.

We all naturally tend at first to believe that the primary qualities in our mental picture do have something corresponding to them in the outer world. In other words, we naturally tend to believe that an outer world does really exist. But, inquires Berkeley, are we justified in believing that an outer world really exists corresponding to the primary qualities of our mental pictures or representations, however natural that belief may be? The belief, he says, may rest on erroneous grounds.

If I were to show you a drawing that somebody had made of your wife or your husband, and were to ask you if it were a good likeness, you would be able to reply, because you are familiar with her or his appearance, and can compare the portrait with the person. But if I were to show you another drawing which I said was a portrait of the Grand Lama of Tibet, and were to ask you if it were a good likeness, then you could not say whether it were so or not, because you do not know what the Grand Lama of Tibet looks like. You cannot compare the portrait with the real person. Further, if I were to show you a third drawing of a young woman, and were to ask you if any real young woman existed of whom the drawing was a portrait, you would have no means of answering me. The only way in which you could tell whether there really existed any young woman corresponding to the portrait would be by knowing her directly, not by knowing only a picture. From the picture, by itself, you could not tell one way or the other whether any such young woman existed, or whether the picture was merely a chocolate-box creation of the artist's with no real young woman corresponding to it.

Now, according to the representative theory of perception all that you can ever experience is the picture you have in your mind. You cannot experience anything else. Consequently, says Berkeley, (and very logically) you cannot tell whether anything exists outside your mind corresponding to that picture inside it. We have no reason at all for believing that anything whatever exists independently, corresponding to those ideas, as we can call them, which exist in our minds. The ideas do indubitably exist in our minds. Our moment to moment experience, which is a complex of ideas in our minds (according to this theory) indubitably exists, but we have no ground whatever for believing that anything else exists. In order to know that an outer real world exists, we should have to know it directly, so that we could compare it with the mental picture, and the theory in question expressly denies that any such direct knowledge of a real world is possible. To think that any independently real world exists (apart from the pictures in our minds which constitute our experience) is, says Berkeley, merely a vulgar superstition from which it is the work of philosophy to emancipate us.

So, according to Berkeley, the real state of affairs is altogether different from what we used to think, and is indeed the opposite of it. We used to think that there existed a real world of material things, mountains, oceans, tables, chairs and human bodies, and that there also existed human minds, these minds having ideas in them which picture that external real world of material things, some parts of the complex of ideas in our minds (the primary qualities) being like the corresponding primary qualities in the external world, while other parts of the complex of ideas (the secondary qualities) have no such counterparts in the external world. But now, says Berkeley, we must as a consequence of our ruminating over these problems abandon that venerable superstition, and recognize that nothing at all exists except minds, each mind having its own private ideas in it.

You may or may not agree with this view, but at least it is understandable, provided that you see how Berkeley advanced step by step until he arrived at his very remarkable conclusion.

There is a further and even odder conclusion which the remorselessly logical will proceed to draw, although Berkeley himself did not do so. If you agree that there is no independently existing real world, but only ideas in your mind, what about animals and persons? Are they also only ideas in your mind? If you agree, for instance, that this book, like the tables and the chairs, is only a complex of sensations and ideas in your mind, what about me who wrote it? If you are to be strictly logical, I too must exist only as an idea in your mind, so that when you do not think of me I do not exist. I too am 'mind-dependent' on you, like pains and sensations of pleasure, for the same reasons that lead you to conclude that the tables and chairs you experience are mind-dependent. This view is known as solipsism, which means literally 'one's-self-alone-ism'. A tale is told of some eccentric who found the argument for solipsism so convincing that he expressed surprise that other people were not solipsists also, but solipsism is a conclusion at which all but the most determined are likely to boggle, and there are few solipsists. Berkeleians, however, can still be found in some universities and technical colleges.

Berkeley was of course very violently criticized by his astonished contemporaries, and many attempted to dismiss his unpalatable conclusion without further inquiry as merely silly. You may feel tempted to do so yourself. You may thump your fist on the table, hurting your knuckles and exclaiming to your companions that it is nonsense to maintain that a hard unyielding table-top exists only as an idea in your mind. This appeal to common sense is however in no way an argument against Berkeley, since he would have accounted satisfactorily for your experience of the hard unyielding table by explaining that what had in fact happened was that a certain succession of ideas had followed one another in your consciousness. The ideas of the table, and yourself and your companions sitting around it, had occurred in your mind and were followed by the idea of thumping the table, and this in turn was followed by the idea or sensation called pain in the knuckles. Berkeley would have said that it was agreed by all concerned that all these ideas or sensations undoubtedly existed in your mind but, he would ask, what evidence does this afford that anything else existed? What evidence is there that the table is part of a public independently-existing real world any more than was the pain? To criticise Berkeley in this way only shows that the critic has failed to grasp Berkeley's main point.

Many objections less naïve than the preceding can of course be made to the Berkeleian view, and of these some will already have sprung to your mind. Why is it, you will ask, that different people have approximately similar ideas at the same time? On Locke's theory there is an explanation for this, namely that there exist external public real objects which cause those similar ideas to occur in different minds at the same time. On Berkeley's view, on the contrary, there is no explanation. On his theory, you and your companion beside the fire are having ideas of a fire and of the room you are sitting in, but there exists no real fire and no real room, and the position is in fact essentially the same as if you were both having toothache at the same time. Your ache is real enough, in one sense. So is your experience of the fire and of the room, but the ache and the fire and the room that you experience are, says Berkeley, private to yourself. Similarly your friend's ache, and the fire and the room that he experiences are private to him. There is no more a publicly existing fire in a publicly existing room than there is a publicly existing toothache. Why then should you and he have similar ideas at the same time? This is a fair question to ask of Berkeley. He replies that it is because God made it so out of his Divine care and beneficence. This amounts to an assertion that it undeniably happens, but that there is no reason for it known to man. This in the end is what Berkeley in effect says, though he adds a defensive tail to his argument by remarking that anyhow his explanation is no worse than that of the materialists, such as Descartes and Locke, who have equal difficulty in finding a reason why external matter possessing only primary qualities could bring into existence secondary qualities.

A further very natural objection to Berkeley that most people make, before they have fully thought out what he said, is to ask what on his view becomes of things when nobody thinks about them. Does the map on the wall behind me pop into existence whenever I think of it, and pop out of existence again when I turn my attention elsewhere and cease to think of it? Berkeley could have pointed out in reply that this objection was irrelevant, because it had assumed the point at issue. It is only if we have already assumed that objects are real things existing in a public independent world that we have any grounds for complaining about the discontinuity which Berkeley's theory involves. This would be a logical reply, but for some reason, Berkeley as well as making this reply, made another one also. He said that objects which are for the time being unperceived by us continue to exist as ideas in the mind of God. This argument constitutes an unnecessary confusion of his own making, since the idea which continues to exist in the mind of God is not the same as the idea which ceases to exist in my mind. If, therefore, the idea of the map ceases to exist in my mind (which is what is meant by saying that I no longer think of the map), then that idea of the map has ceased to exist, whether or not there exists at the same time some other idea in the mind of God. That other idea in the mind of God would no doubt be an idea of a map also, but it would be a different idea in a different mind. Berkeley's argument here is either a mystery or else contradictory of his own main thesis. In this interpretation, of course, we are taking as being his main thesis the one which is most important for our purposes. It may have been that Berkeley's own personal interests were primarily in a semi-mystical doctrine of the existence of all things ' in God '. The point for us is that the alleged explanation is not an explanation of the difficulty which it purports to solve. It is thoroughly confused, and has made the understanding of Berkeley unduly difficult for his readers.

On the whole, however, Berkeley was able to make quite logical rebuttals of most of his critics, simply by pointing out that his conclusion followed logically, if unpalatably, from premises which the critics shared with him.

I expect that the outcome of this introduction to Berkeley is that you are now saying somewhat doubtfully to yourself : ' This is all very well. It seems to follow quite logically, step by step, from what went before. Berkeley seems to be right enough—and yet I just do not believe it.' If that is the way it strikes you, I think you are right. It is what I think about it myself.

CHAPTER VI
Berkeley's Contribution

W E are now in a bewildering position. What does this all mean? What are we to think next ?

Well, what does a scientist do when something like this happens to him, as it very frequently does in narrower fields? Think of the situation in which Einstein found himself with reference to Newton's Laws of Motion in physics. Einstein's procedure amounted to saying that if Newton's theory is sound, then we can take the next step and deduce from his theory what the movements of the planets are going to be. We can deduce, for example, where Mercury will be at a given time. (This, as can be demonstrated, is an inescapable consequence of Newton's Laws of Motion, in the same way as Berkeley's view of the universe is an inescapable consequence of the representative theory.) When, however, the astronomers in the observatories looked through their telescopes at Mercury at the time specified, they saw that it was not in the place where, on Newton's theory, it ought to have been. It was observably in a different place. It was not very far away from the expected place, but it was definitely not in it. Einstein was therefore in much the same position with reference to Newton's theory as we are in with reference to Berkeley's theory.

Einstein did not deal with this by saying that there was something wrong with the telescopes, nor did he regard the situation as an insoluble puzzle and give up. Instead he argued that if it follows from Newton's Laws of Motion that Mercury should be in such and such a place at such and such a time, and if Mercury is not in that place at that time, then there must be something wrong with Newton's Laws of Motion.

There is nothing particularly scientific in this procedure. There is not even anything unusual in it, for it is a procedure we all carry out many times a day. Suppose that I want to find out which fuse in the fuse-box controls the electric light in my bedroom. I think I know which one, and so I remove the fuse in question, but I find that the light in my bedroom is not affected. I then say that the fuse does not control that light. In doing this, I do not explicitly formulate an argument to myself, saying: ' If my view or theory that this fuse controls my bedroom light is sound, then when I remove the fuse the light will not shine. But I find that the light does shine, therefore there is something wrong with my theory that this fuse controls my bedroom light. I must therefore try another fuse.' Of course I do not formulate the argument explicitly in this way, but what I am doing is exactly the same procedure on a small scale that Einstein carried out on a large scale. It is a way in which everybody argues, scientists, philosophers and all.

We, in our position, have now to do the same with the theory on which we have been working. Here we have had under review the theory that all we can experience are representations or mental pictures, or sensations, or ideas, or whatever else we may loosely call them, in our minds, and that we cannot know material things directly. Berkeley deduced, as a consequence of this, that no material things exist in the universe, but only minds —my mind, your mind, the next man's mind, each of us shut up in his own mind with his own ' mental pictures ', there being no common public world existing independently. (This consequence follows from the representationist theory in the same way as it follows from Newton's Laws of Motion that Mercury would be in a specified place at a specified time.)

Now in the same way as Einstein found that the

consequences he deduced from Newton's Laws of Motion were contrary to fact, and could not be believed, so the consequences which Berkeley deduced from the representationist theory appear also to be contrary to fact. Berkeley's consequence follows logically from the representationist theory, but it cannot be believed. Therefore, precisely as Einstein concluded that there must be something wrong with Newton's theory, so we conclude that there must be something wrong with the representationist theory. There must be something wrong with the theory that we cannot know the real world directly and that we know only mental representations existing in our minds only.

The parallel drawn here for purposes of exposition between Einstein's treatment of the Newtonian physics and our treatment, by means of Berkeley, of the representative theory of perception, is not of course complete in all respects. Einstein's treatment of Newton was not to produce an entirely different theory, but to adapt the former theory to account for the new evidence which had accumulated since Newton's day. Our treatment of the representationist theory, on the other hand, will be to abandon it entirely, and to work out an alternative which is different. The parallelism is referred to here only to explain the method of argument.

The conclusion to which we have been brought by Berkeley is his contribution to the advancement of philosophy. He showed, once and for all, that if anybody attempts to explain how material things exist and how we know them, by holding that we know mental representations of them, then he is next compelled to hold that there exist no such things at all, but only minds with sensations or ideas in them. He is compelled to hold that there exists no common public world of real things, and that mountains and railway engines are no more independently real entities than are toothaches. This is a conclusion we cannot accept, so that the original theory from which that conclusion is deduced must itself be abandoned.

This result is not at all the outcome to which Berkeley had hoped that his work would lead. It appears that his intention had been to refute all materialists, but for this purpose his work was irrelevant. Materialism may well be refutable, as I believe it is, but not by Berkeley's arguments. If this was his intention, he failed, but in so doing he advanced us all bodily forward in our understanding of the problems of knowledge. In philosophy, as in so much else, the most valuable and enduring products of any planned activity sometimes turn out to be the by-products.

At this point the character of the discussion changes. Up to this point the reader has been led through a very much foreshortened summary of the intellectual experiences which come to every student when he begins the serious study of philosophy. The account I have given up to this point is one with which most contemporary philosophers would more or less agree, provided that they make allowance for the shortness of the available space. But from this point onwards the book consists mainly of an outline of my own views on the question of the nature of knowledge. This alternative to the representationist view stated and criticized in the first part of the book is given here primarily to entice or incite the new reader of philosophy into reading more philosophy elsewhere. If it disturbs to some degree the reader's acceptance of his present views, and leads him to further reading and meditation, it will have served its purpose.[1] This being so, it, unlike the first part, does

---

[1] The statement given here is no more than an outline. For a fuller exposition the reader must be asked to wait for the publication of the manuscript referred to in the Preface as *The Owl of Minerva*.

not outline a view to which every student normally comes, but instead outlines a view which is only one of many possible alternatives. This view appears to me to offer the best prospect, and perhaps the only prospect, of understanding the problems with which we now find ourselves faced, but it is not a view with which the majority of contemporary philosophers would agree. I must make this clear to the reader, lest he should accept what I say as representing the consensus of opinion among contemporary philosophers, which it does not. In this second part, even more than in the first, the reader must work out his conclusions for himself.

It is arguable, and with reason, that matter such as that of the second part of this book should not be included in an introductory book, especially as the statement of it must in the circumstances be inevitably inadequate. On the other hand, I am here mainly concerned to make the reader experience what it feels like to think philosophically, and I believe that he is more likely to have this experience if he is given for his consideration a view that is genuinely open to dispute and in fact is disputed. This second part has therefore been included in the hope of giving the reader the experience of being presented with one proposed alternative to the views rejected in the first part, and of considering that alternative for himself on something like level terms with the writer.

Bearing these repetitious warnings in mind, let us now take stock of the position we have reached. The preceding argument concerning the Berkeleian consequences of the representative theory of perception was reasonably straightforward and clear. There was no special subtlety in it, and no exceptional penetration is required to follow it. It merely shows what happens to any thinker who sets out from the simple representationist theory of the way in which we perceive material objects around us. It shows that the theory will not work. As such, the argument is comparatively limited in its scope. But underlying it, there are issues of vastly wider importance. These are, indeed, of fundamental importance, not merely to the understanding of our knowledge of material objects, but to the understanding of our knowledge of all things, material and otherwise. This requires considerably more acumen to appreciate. It is these issues which we are now going on to deal with, and it is mainly because of them that the Berkeleian argument has been worth studying.

Consider the situation in this way. The representationist theory was formulated by certain seventeenth-century philosophers. To them it appeared reasonable, and it appears reasonable to us when it is explained to us to-day. Now, no person is likely to invent this theory out of nothing at all, and we to-day are certainly not likely to think it reasonable unless there were already in us something predisposing us to accept it. This suggests that there probably already is something in the outlook that we, as members of the same civilization, share with them, with which it is compatible or from which it follows.

I believe that there is (though this is highly controversial), and I believe that this consists of an even more deep-seated, and even less recognized, presupposition about the nature of knowledge. (This is the 'wider issue' referred to above.) This is the assumption that, in knowing, there are involved three factors: namely, first the knower, second his ideas or concepts or the like of the real world, and third the real world itself. We shall call this for convenience the 'three factor assumption'. The statement probably appears a very flat platitude to you, but this is because you already tacitly hold that assumption, although without being aware of doing so. This assumption is very widely held in our Western civilization.

At this point the reader will probably complain, with some justification, that these present paragraphs are vague and obscure. This is mainly because the underlying assumption about which I am writing is so unquestioningly accepted by us all that we do not notice it, any more than we notice the air we breathe. It is only when we begin to breathe a different kind of air that our attention is drawn to it by the contrast. In much the same way it is only when we become acquainted with a different theory of knowledge that we even begin to be clear about the assumption we had so long unquestioningly held. You will therefore find that as we go on to outline an alternative theory, the assumptions we have previously held become clearer. (This will be noticeably so in the later discussion of the nature of language.) Therefore, if this discussion of this very fundamental presupposition is at the moment not very clear, read slowly on. The point is an exceedingly subtle one, and my own experience has been that it only gradually becomes clear.

Although this presupposition, which I have called the ' three term ' presupposition as to the nature of knowledge, has been widely and hitherto almost unquestioningly held by all but a very few philosophers, this does not mean that all who share that presupposition have the same philosophies. On the contrary, different philosophers have worked out very different and in many cases apparently contradictory philosophies from that same basis. The point is that these various philosophies, however different, still fall within the limits laid down by that underlying presupposition. When, for instance, the philosophers of the seventeenth and eighteenth centuries came to deal with the problems of the nature of knowledge in terms of this underlying assumption which they all shared, some of them, such as Locke and Berkeley, were impressed mainly by the importance of sensory experience, and in consequence worked out the theory we know as simple representationism. Others, such as Leibniz and Spinoza,[1] were impressed by the unreliability of sensory experience and by the importance of those ideas which appeared to be independent of sensory experience, such as the concepts of mathematics. These two types of philosopher appear to be radically different, and in consequence they are generally classified in the histories of philosophy as respectively the ' English Empiricists ' and the ' Continental Rationalists '. The differences between these various philosophers are of course in many ways very important. Similarly the differences among those of the more modern and contemporary philosophers who further develop the same philosophies are important also. For us, however, who are at the moment concerned with the fundamental problem of the nature of knowledge, these differences are in comparison irrelevant, as we are concerned not with their opinions on this or that particular point, but with the very fundamental and mostly unquestioned assumption upon which the several views of nearly

[1] Gottfried Wilhelm Leibniz (1646–1716). Mathematician (inventor independently of Newton of the differential and integral calculus), philosopher, politician and diplomatic representative of the Holy Roman Empire. Published in the *Monadology* an outline of his philosophy, which is largely the application to philosophical problems of the scientific advances of his own time, on a basis of the underlying representationist presupposition as to the nature of knowledge.

Baruch (or Benedict) Spinoza (1632–1677). Philosopher and practical optician. Appears to have been a singularly saintly and lovable person. Excommunicated and cursed in form by the Jewish community of Amsterdam, his home, for his pantheistic and heterodox opinions. His philosophy, as in his *Tractatus Theologico-politicus* and his *Ethics*, was largely the application of the contemporary mathematical and scientific outlook to the problems of theology and ethics on a Cartesian basis.

all of them rest, namely the assumption that in knowing there are involved the knower, his ideas or concepts, and the real world. The bulk of modern philosophy, in its innumerable divergent forms, is still based on that assumption.

The position, put briefly once again, is that it appears to me that any theory of knowledge based upon that presupposition is misleading and ought to be abandoned, for reasons analogous to those outlined in the first pages of this chapter when discussing the simple and almost naïve exemplification of it commonly called the representative theory of perception. Again I must in fairness emphasize that my view is not commonly held by contemporary philosophers. Most contemporary philosophy appears to me still to be working out the consequences in one form or another of the primitive, and I believe fundamentally misleading, presupposition that in knowing there are involved the knower, his ideas (under whatever name), and real things. For that reason I believe that there will be no major advance in philosophic understanding until that assumption and all its consequences are abandoned. Berkeley's unwitting contribution has been that he has shown the lines on which a refutation of it can be formulated.

This is a very large issue, over which the reader will demand time to think, but fortunately it is possible to continue this introduction profitably without having to make up one's mind at this stage on this extremely subtle and difficult question. On this, as on all deeper philosophical questions, we do not ' make up our minds ' point by point. Instead, we go on thinking over the question, sometimes forgetting it, and then one day discover that our minds appear to have made themselves up. In other words, a fuller understanding comes, a little to our surprise, with time. The reader can therefore go on with some prospect of not feeling left for ever in mid-air.

CHAPTER VII

Finding a Better Alternative

W E have now reached the position of concluding, if you agree with me, that somehow or other we know the real world directly, and not at second hand. What we know is the real world, and our knowledge of the world around us is not a vast illusion, as we were at one time led by Descartes and Locke and others to believe.

This conclusion, however, though no doubt clear so far as it goes, still leaves an enormous problem untouched. It throws no light at all on the plain fact that different people have different experiences of the same situation, and that we make mistakes and know that we make mistakes. If we simply knew the real world directly, and if that were the whole story, then we should all have the same experience, and no one could ever make a mistake. Clearly the situation is much more complex than this. Our problem is therefore to work out an alternative theory which will take account of these complexities. It must explain how different people in the same situation can have genuinely different experiences, while also explaining how knowledge can be direct and not representative. This alternative will be the topic of the following chapters.

Hereupon a new difficulty arises to plague us both. Even though you may have agreed with me in explicitly rejecting the representative view, you are still very much influenced by it. This is natural and inevitable, and in itself is not by any means discreditable. You cannot change the intellectual habits of your previous lifetime in a moment, and you will for some time continue to think in terms of the representative theory, even though you may have explicitly rejected it. You may reject it when it is explicitly stated as a theory, but it will remain for some time as an assumption ' at the back of your mind ', and as such will continue to lay down the limits within which will fall all your opinions concerning the theory of knowledge. Changes in such deep-seated assumptions can only come gradually.

If I now try to outline to you some alternative theory of knowledge, I shall of course have to do so in terms of that new alternative theory itself, because what I write will not make sense in any other way. At first you will interpret what I write in terms of the old familiar representative view. The consequence is that if I were now to begin a systematic exposition, you would find yourself at once regarding it as either incomprehensible or wrong, for the very good reason that, *on the representative theory whose lingering influence still affects you*, the new alternative view would not make sense. This constitutes a special disability which makes the study of the theory of knowledge peculiarly difficult. We all suffer from it.

The best and indeed the only way that I can think of to circumvent this very real difficulty is to begin not by a systematic and definitive exposition, but by a discussion intended to do no more than give the reader some first hint of the alternative theory that I have in mind. Thereafter, as we advance, the theory will I hope become by stages progressively clearer.

For this purpose, and in this manner, let us turn our attention once more to our sense-organs. When we consider how they detect things in our environment, the point that at once impresses us is how little they do in fact detect. Consider our eyes. The retinas of the eyes detect light-waves as do the sensitized films in cameras. As the scientists would put it, they react to light-waves, i.e. to electromagnetic vibrations of a certain range of wavelength. They do not react to other electro-magnetic vibrations which are either longer or shorter in wave-length than light-waves, though otherwise similar ; and there are innumerable other such electro-magnetic vibrations all around us at all times.

This is a somewhat surprising fact of which comparatively few people seem to be aware. Take an analogy to make it clearer. Suppose that you are on board ship, and that you lean over the side and look down at the waves. There is not only one sort of wave on the surface of the water, but many sorts. Some of them are very large and very long, the distance from the crest of one wave to the crest of the next being about the length of the ship. If you are in mid-ocean there may even be still longer waves, the deep sea swell, which are so long that you cannot easily pick out the crests by the eye, though you can feel their presence by the slow rise and fall of the whole ship. In addition to those very long waves there are all sorts of smaller waves also, the distance from the crest of one to the crest of the next being a matter of yards or feet. There are also still smaller wavelets chasing each other over the surface of the water hither and thither, some of them so small that the distance from the crest of one to the crest of the next may be only a fraction of an inch. All those different waves, of such widely differing wave-lengths, are passing hither and thither over the surface of the water all the time.

Something very similar to this is happening in the room in which you are now sitting, the waves in this case being electro-magnetic waves such as light-waves and wireless waves. Passing through the room hither and thither at enormous velocities, and passing through your body also, are electro-magnetic waves of innumerable different lengths. Some are very long indeed, so long that the crest of one wave is miles away from the crest of the next. Others are so short that the crest of one is only a most minute fraction of a millimetre away from the next. There are all sorts of others whose lengths fall in between these extremes. They are all there. They are all in the room, i.e. passing through the room, at the instant at which you are reading this.

Some of them, but only a very few of them, are of such a length that they affect your eyes. If an electro-magnetic wave is shorter than about 1/30,000 of an inch, and longer than about 1/60,000 of an inch, then it affects the retina. When waves between these upper and lower limits are reflected by objects and fall on the eye, they cause changes in the retina, and this in turn causes changes in the nerves behind the eye, which in turn cause changes in the brain ; after which, in some way· we do not understand, we have the experience we call ' seeing '. For that reason, waves between those upper and lower limits of length are called ' visible ', or ' light-waves '.

There are also other electro-magnetic waves passing through the room, which are exactly like these, only somewhat longer. They do not affect the retina, but they do affect certain nerve-endings in the skin. They cause nerve-currents to pass along nerves from the skin to the brain, and after these reach the brain we have the experience we call ' feeling heat '. If somebody thoughtfully provides a hot drink for you at bed-time, then the glass will not be visible if you switch out your bedside light, but you will be able to feel the heat of it on your hand when you bring your hand close to it. This is because the heated liquid is emitting waves of the lengths that affect the heat-sensitive organs in your skin, but is not emitting the very slightly shorter waves which would affect the retinas of your eyes. There are yet other electro-magnetic waves also, which are exactly the same except that they are longer still. They do not affect the body at all. Then there are others even longer, which do not affect the body, but do affect wireless receiving sets. These are called 'radio-frequencies' or 'wireless waves'. We are familiar with the lengths of such waves from reading the dials on any wireless set. All these different waves are round about us at all times, even though our sense-organs fail to detect them. If you had a wireless set beside you at this moment, and were slowly to turn the tuning knob, you would hear one station after the other. All those stations are sending their waves through the room, and through your body, at this moment, but none of them caused any reaction in your body, and you would not have known they were there at all, unless you had used the wireless set to detect them. Your sense-organs themselves do not detect them.

Not only are there in the room around you those waves which you cannot detect because they are longer than those to which your sense-organs react; there are also innumerable other waves which you do not detect because they are shorter than those to which your sense-organs react, such as ultra-violet rays, gamma-rays, and others.

The point of this long string of examples is to emphasize how very small is the range of electro-magnetic waves which are detected by our sense-organs. If the range of wave-lengths known to the scientists were represented by a line from the top to the bottom of this page, then the part of that range that our sense-organs detect—namely light-waves and heat-waves—would be represented by a section of the line too small to see except with a magnifying glass.

So, speaking picturesquely and loosely, our eyes are blind to very nearly all that surrounds us. We can console ourselves for this deficiency by the consideration that it is well that things are so, because otherwise we should no doubt be hopelessly confused. It appears to be only because our eyes are blind to very nearly everything, because they neglect very nearly everything, that we are able to see things around us as we do. If our eyes detected more, we should then no doubt experience only confusion, something analogous to the confusion we experience at present if we listen to an unsatisfactory wireless set which reacts at the same time not only to one wave-length but to neighbouring wave-lengths also. This produces a jumble of sounds, with one programme on top of another. If our eyes were not blind to all but a very limited range of wave-lengths, we might well have a similar sort of confusion in our visual experience. (The reader will at this point probably inquire what is meant by calling our normal daily experience 'orderly' as distinguished from that possible state of confusion. Is there, he may ask, any independent standard of what constitutes confusion, or is what we call 'order' only that kind of confusion with which we have grown familiar and with which we are consequently able to cope? This is the kind of question that will or will not appear significant to the reader according to the amount of questioning thought that he has given to the matter. We shall return to this opinion later in a context that will make the point more clear.)

The same considerations apply to hearing, except of course that the waves are waves in air, and not electro-magnetic waves. At the present moment there are air waves of all sorts of wave-lengths passing to and fro in the air of the room you are in. They are falling on the drums of your ears. If these air-waves are longer than about thirty-five feet you cannot hear them. If they are shorter than about seven-eighths of an inch you cannot hear them. Dogs, as you probably know, can hear sounds that human beings cannot hear, because dog's ears react to sound-waves shorter than those to which human ears react. Poachers become applied scientists in this connexion, for they make whistles which produce air-waves just long enough to make a dog's ears react, but not long enough to make the game-keeper's ears react.

So, again speaking picturesquely and loosely, our ears are deaf to very nearly everything, just as our eyes are blind to very nearly everything. The same applies to all our other sense-organs. They react to only minute sections of all that surrounds them, and do not react to the vast remainder. In this way they may be said to select for our attention only very minute sections of our environment, very minute sections indeed.

If you have already read some modern writings on the theory of knowledge you may at this point find yourself saying ' But the sensa or sensibilia are not selected. They are somehow created ', and if you have not read any such writings you may find yourself raising the same objection by saying that our sensations are not selected but created. This is an instance of that slipping back into a representationist way of thinking, or ' three-term ' theory of knowledge, of which I spoke as a perpetual plague at the beginning of the chapter. The objection is one which can quite logically be made if we hold a representationist view, but not otherwise. Whether we do hold a representationist view or not is another question. I believe that we can not, for the reasons outlined in chapter VI, while others may think differently, but the point here is that if we make the above objection, we have thereby tacitly assumed the representationist view. The reason for emphasizing this at length is that many writers tend to make the above objection while at the same time maintaining and believing themselves to have abandoned the representationist way of thinking.

Now, in the light of all this, let us take stock. As

a result of thinking along with Berkeley, and as a result of the change in our thinking which he brought about, and as a result of our further cogitation on the points in this chapter, we now find ourselves taking a view which is the opposite of that held by philosophers like Descartes and Locke.

They held that the real world was somewhat dull and uninteresting, and that the secondary qualities, the warmth and colour of our daily experience, had no real counterparts, but were merely something added to our own private mental pictures. They thought, indeed, that the richness of our experience was an illusion, and that there existed nothing real corresponding to it.

We now have come to a view which is precisely the opposite, namely that the real world is almost unbelievably rich and complicated, so complicated that we should be confused and bewildered if we experienced anything more than minute and much simplified selections from it. What we experience (that is to say the world as we know it in ordinary day-to-day experience) is only a fragmentary selection of the real world; and we experience such minute selections as we do experience because our sense-organs react to them only, and are blind and deaf and unfeeling to all the vast remainder.

Let us now consider more fully what is involved in the preceding. Suppose—to take a fanciful but not necessarily misleading analogy, though still speaking somewhat loosely—that there is a large aerial fixed up outside your house, with the lead-in coming through the window and the end of the wire lying loose on a table. Let us have some friends in to see you, and let us fall to discussing what programme is, as people say, ' coming down ' the lead-in. Suppose that I have with me a very simple little wireless set of my own. It has no adjustable tuning device, but has fixed tuning, and is so made that it will react to the B.B.C. Home Service wave-length and to no other. It has no loud-speaker, but only earphones, so that I can hear it, while none of the others can. When I pick up the lead-in, and touch the wire against the proper terminal on my little set, I say : ' It's the B.B.C. Home Service that is coming down the lead-in ', for that is what I hear. In the room there is another friend of yours who also has his own little set. It is exactly like mine, only it is tuned to the B.B.C. Forces Programme. He picks up the lead-in, touches it to his set and says : ' No, it's the Forces Programme '. Let us also have an American visitor in the room, with a set tuned to the Boston short-wave station in his own country. He puts the lead-in on to his set, and he says : ' No, you are both wrong. The programme coming down this lead-in is the programme of the Boston short-wave station.'

If we three then asked you to explain to us this apparently incomprehensible situation, you could do so quite easily. You would explain to us that these different programmes were all of them coming down the lead-in, and that each of us could hear only the one to which he was himself tuned. You would explain that what was coming down the lead-in was in reality extremely complicated, and that the wireless set that each of us was using served to pick out for each of us from that complicated congestion only one particular range of electro-magnetic vibrations. You would explain that each of us was unaware of the other ranges of wave-lengths, because each of us had only his own wireless set, permanently tuned to just one range of wave-lengths. You would add that there were innumerable other ranges of wave-lengths also, such as those radiated by the various Continental stations, by ships and aircraft, and so forth, all of which were coming down the lead-in as well, though nobody in the room detected any of them, because nobody in the room had a set tuned to any of them.

This is a somewhat grotesque situation to imagine, but it makes quite a good analogy to explain the situation in which you and I and all men are, in our daily experience. There are surrounding us at this moment what can be described as innumerable electro-magnetic vibrations, of innumerably different wave-lengths, to nearly all of which we are blind, and similarly there are innumerable air-waves of innumerably different wave-lengths, to nearly all of which we are deaf.

Only the most minute sections of them are of the lengths to which our eyes and ears and other sense-organs are tuned, and the experience we call ' seeing and hearing and feeling the things around us ', is simply the experience that arises from the reaction of our sense-organs to that very minute section, while the vast remainder is neglected. That remainder is all there too, even though our sense-organs do not react to it, much as in our analogy all the programmes were, as we say, coming down that lead-in, though we each reacted to and were aware of only one of them, while not reacting to and not being aware of the others.

This analogy is admittedly an over-statement of the differences between the experiences that different men have. It is an over-statement of the differences between what the sense-organs of one man detect and what the sense-organs of another man detect. These differences are in fact *comparatively* small. It is, however, by no means an over-statement of the differences between what the sense-organs of men react to and what the sense-organs of animals and insects react to. Insects and butterflies and bees, for instance, have eyes that react to electro-magnetic vibrations whose lengths are fairly near the lengths that human eyes react to, but the range of lengths to which they react is not by any means the same. In some cases they react to longer waves, in some cases to shorter. Bees in particular are very remarkable, for the retinas of their eyes change with the seasons, and in late autumn they react to a range of electromagnetic vibrations which is measurably different from the range to which they react in spring. Moreover, at one period of the year, there is, in the middle of the range of vibrations to which they do react, a gap to which they do not react.

This line of thought leads to an explanation of that puzzle which we used as a means of starting our inquiry, namely that the men we call colour-blind see only one uniform colour in two lights, while you and I see two different colours. The fact that a colour-blind man sees no difference in two lights which to us look conspicuously different makes us think at first that that his eyes must be very unlike ours. Yet, though his eyes are not quite the same as ours, they are not by any means as different from ours as are, say, the eyes of a bee. The colour-blind man's difference from people of normal colour vision is comparatively small. The explanation of his different experience appears to be as follows.

The waves, or what can be described as the waves, which cause you and me to see what we call red, are longer than the waves that cause us to see what we call green, but only very slightly longer, only by about $1/120,000$ of an inch. Our retinas react to the longer waves in a way which is different from the way in which they react to waves $1/120,000$ inch shorter, and hence we have different experiences, i.e. we see different colours. The colour-blind man's retina is not so discriminating. It reacts in the same way to both sets of waves. Hence he sees only one colour, no matter whether it be the longer or the shorter waves that are falling upon his retina. Probably he sees the world around him much as normal people see an etching or a drawing, rather than as they see a coloured painting.

To sum up the outcome of this stage of our inquiry, it is beginning to appear that we do experience reality directly, yet that different people can have different experiences because, owing to the nature of our sense-organs, we do not experience anything like the whole of reality, but only some astonishingly small scraps of it, there being in some cases different scraps for different people.

We have therefore passed far beyond the theory of Descartes and Locke that the real world is simple, bare and colourless, and that we each add the richness of colour and warmth and all the other secondary qualities to the private and largely illusory picture that each of us has in his own mind. Instead, we have now come to the opposite, and incidentally much pleasanter, conclusion that the real world is astonishingly rich and complex, containing genuinely in itself all those interesting qualities which Descartes and Locke believed were illusions. The real world *is* what I experience it to be. It is also what you experience it to be, and what the next man experiences it to be; and what the colour-blind man experiences it to be; and what animals and insects experience it to be; and a very great deal more also. The reason why we have different experiences is not that each of us has a private and subjective picture, but that each of us picks out and attends to only a part of the immensely rich and complex world in which we find ourselves, and one man's part may not be the same as another man's part.

By this time an alternative theory has begun to emerge, or in other words an alternative way of looking upon the question of the nature of knowledge is becoming possible. It must, however, be specifically noted that this alternative theory is no more than suggested; and, further, that the argument by which it has been suggested cannot be used as a proof, because the means I have used to suggest it is observation of the working of our sense-organs, and our sense-organs are themselves observed by us in precisely the same way as are tables and chairs, and are subject to the same qualifications. Whatever the conclusions that we come to about tables and chairs and how we know them, we must hold the same conclusions about our sense-organs themselves and about the way we know them. We must not fall into the capacious trap, into which so many amateur philosophers fall, of thinking that we can produce a theory of knowledge by arguing from the working of the sense-organs, and forgetting that in so doing they may have contradicted the suppositions underlying the view they take of our knowledge of those quite material objects, namely our own sense-organs, on which the new alleged theory is based.

CHAPTER VIII

'Selecting' and 'Grouping'

I T would be comparatively simple if we 'knew' or experienced everything to which our sense-organs react; but we do not. Complex processes of the kind we call mental take place, through which only a part of that to which our sense-organs react is in fact experienced by us. These mental processes are extremely difficult to examine, but they can be roughly described as ways of paying attention. They settle how much is attended to, and in what ways.

These mental processes are different in kind from the workings of the sense-organs, which are physical and physiological processes and can be inspected and measured in laboratories. These mental processes cannot be inspected in that way, and therefore we cannot venture to make statements about them nearly as definite as those which we can make with fair certainty about the working of the eyes and ears. We can come to conclusions about them only in an apparently roundabout way. All that we can do to justify the accounts we give of these processes is to say that something more or less like our description must take place, because if it did not, then the experiences we have would not be what in fact they are.

This method of investigation is not a strange and unusual one used only on special subjects such as these obscure and complex mental processes. It is a method used explicitly by scientists and others on all problems other than the simplest. When, for instance, Einstein was working on his relativity physics, and was producing theories about space-time, he could not say : 'I inspect space-time and I observe it to be so-and-so.' Where the sense-organs are concerned, on the other hand, he could of course have inquired more directly. He could have said : 'I inspect the human ear, and I observe it to have an arrangement of bony levers in the middle of it.' Space-time cannot be inspected in that direct way. What Einstein could however say about space-time, and what in effect he did say, was : 'Space-time must be so-and-so, because if it were not, then certain observed facts would not be what they are, e.g. light-rays at an eclipse of the sun would not be bent to such and such a degree, as in fact they are.' This method of investigation is used by everybody, scientists and all, in many of the affairs of daily life. We are perhaps most clearly aware of our following this method where the estimating of human character is concerned. We do not say : 'I have inspected X and I observe him to be patient and tolerant.' It is very difficult to detect patience and tolerance by inspection. Instead we say : 'X must be patient and tolerant, otherwise he wouldn't have put up with Y all these years.'

In the same way, we cannot say : 'I inspect the mental processes under discussion, and I observe them to be so-and-so.' We can only say : 'Something more or less like my description must take place, because if it did not, then certain observed facts of my experience would not be what they are, e.g. unless something more or less like my description takes place, I could not think of the striking of a match as the cause of its lighting, which in fact I do.' Immanuel Kant,[1] to whom so much of this stage of

[1] Immanuel Kant (1724–1804). Lived most of his long life quietly as a university teacher in Königsberg, where he produced *The Critique of Pure Reason* and *The Critique of Judgement*, which revolutionized the theory of knowledge. The quickening influence upon him was Hume.

David Hume (1711–1776). Principal philosophical writings are his *Treatise of Human Nature*, his *Enquiry Concerning Human Understanding*, and his *Dialogues Concerning Natural*

philosophic development is due, gave this proceeding a very long name. He called it ' The Transcendental Deduction of the Categories '; but whatever name he called it, the preceding is what in substance it amounts to.

There is also an obvious practical difference between these mental processes and the workings of the sense-organs. We cannot alter the structure of the retinas of our eyes to make them react to ranges of electro-magnetic vibrations to which at present they do not react. We cannot alter the structure of our ears to make them react to air-waves to which at present they do not react. The mental processes on the other hand are in some ways and to some extent alterable and controllable, in so far as they depend on what interests us, and on what purposes we have in view.

To understand these mental processes, I have found that as good a way as any is to regard them as of two main kinds, which I call ' selecting ' and ' grouping '. This is only a very rough first attempt at a description of them, but these names will serve as convenient labels to let us get started. I do not of course mean that there is one kind of process called ' selecting ', and another altogether different and separate process called ' grouping '. These two names are merely preliminary labels, and in many cases we may find that the same process can be described equally properly as the one or as the other.

Further, I do not mean that these processes of ' selecting ' and ' grouping ' are conscious decisions happening one after the other in time. The whole

Religion, which last is a discussion of the theory of design in nature. Equally known in his own day as an historian. Rotund both in body and in character, and one of the most powerful intellects that the human species has produced. Appears to have enjoyed the liking and respect of even his most indignant philosophic and theological opponents.

process happens without our being aware of it, and must indeed all have happened before we are aware of anything. It is only the results that we are conscious of. The only way, however, in which we can intelligibly discuss these processes at this preliminary stage, owing to the limitations of language, to say nothing of deeper difficulties, is to do so as if the sense-organs first react to some small scraps of the multitudinous influences that surround us, and that we then select for attention some few of these scraps, and then group these few together in various ways. We can at least hope in this way to give an account of the process of knowing which will enable us to understand more or less what is going on when we have experience, and to avoid being grossly misled (as outlined in Chapter II) by our misconceptions as to the nature of knowledge.

Let us take some examples. While you have been reading this book, you have been paying attention to the print upon it, i.e. to variations in the pattern of black and white upon the pages, but you have not paid attention to variations in the texture of the paper, and to the small marks that have come by accident here and there upon the paper. Light-rays reflected by these variations in texture and by these marks have been falling upon the retinas of your eyes just as much as have the light-rays reflected by the printed letters, but out of that innumerable collection you selected for attention only those in which you were for the time being interested, namely the printed letters. You neglected the rest, until the run of the discussion drew your attention to some of them. You did not, to begin with, notice the variations in texture. You do notice them now. That is to say, we do at any one time select in some one way, but we might have selected in innumerable other ways, if there had been anything to make us do so. This selecting for attention of only a small part of what our sense-organs react to, and neglecting the rest, is continually going on, on various levels of grossness or subtlety. On a gross level, it is this process that allows of those many tricks of oversight to which we fall victims. The conjurer, for instance, relies upon it when by his patter and by the movements of his right hand he leads his audience not to select for attention the movements of his left hand while it unobtrusively changes the cards or keeps the rabbit quiet in the hat. A very similar procedure is commonly employed in political propaganda, both international and inter-party, and for similar reasons it is commonly successful.

No long string of examples is needed to point out how typical this is of all our experience. It is conspicuous when once it is pointed out, though not until then. The reason why it is not conspicuous until it is pointed out is that on the whole, as far as practical matters are concerned, we all select for attention much the same sorts of things, except in details. It is only when you and I discover that we have been selecting for attention different sorts of things that we realize we have been selecting at all.

The selective process is perhaps most conspicuously shown by the way in which we give an account of any incident. In telling a friend about some happening, we do not pay attention to everything that occurred at the time and place in question, but only to a very small selection which we happen to think important or significant or interesting. This is why it is so often said that a good story-teller is a man who knows what to leave out. In other words, he does his selecting in a very careful and artistic way. He differs from the incompetent story-teller not by selecting, but by the way in which he selects. Everybody has to select. Even bores have to select. They cannot tell you everything that occurred. Human life is too short. Unfortunately they persist in selecting for attention—for their own attention and unfortunately for ours also—only exasperatingly trivial things. Bores are not necessarily the people who talk most. They often do not talk as much as interesting people, but they seem to talk more because they select such uninteresting things to talk about.

The same applies on a bulkier scale to the writing of books. Consider how an historian has to select. An historian writing a history of Britain in the nineteenth century cannot pay attention to everything that happened here in that hundred years. It would take him very much more than a hundred years to do it. What makes him a good historian, if he is one, is that he selects for his own attention, and thus for his readers' attention, what is significant among the events and conditions of the time, leaving the vast remainder entirely neglected. The mere chronicler inevitably selects also, but he is not capable of selecting the significant only. He selects a jumble of the significant and the insignificant. This is why we may read his chronicle without in the end being very much the wiser, whereas if we read the competent historian's history we feel that we have not only gained more information, but have also gained a deeper understanding. (The reader will here inquire what constitutes the significant. We shall return below to this, and to the wider question of which it is a particular case.)

The kinds of things that a man or woman selects for attention, whether in the writing of a standard history or in the chattering of social gossip, give a fairly good indication of what he or she thinks worth while. This is why, after listening to some one for some time, you may or may not have learned very much about the subject under discussion, but you will have learned a good deal about what sort of person the speaker is.

It would be disproportionate to attempt here a catalogue of the different ways in which we thus 'select'. I am using these examples to show that this 'selecting' does in fact take place when we experience the world we live in; or rather, that it has already taken place without our being aware of it, for it is only *because* this selecting has taken place that the world we experience appears to us as it does. If we 'selected' different things, then the world we experience would be different.

At this point a question like that concerning the 'significant' but of wider importance has I hope arisen acutely in your mind. If I select for attention one sort of thing, and you select for attention a different sort of thing, is one of us right, and the other wrong? Or, to put the question less extremely, is one way better than the other, and if so, which? This is a question we shall return to later, after dealing with 'grouping', in connection with which the same question will arise.

As to the process I have called 'grouping', take an example to illustrate what is meant. Think of standing beside the sea and watching the waves coming in. A crest comes, followed by a trough, then another crest and another trough, and so on. Has it ever occurred to you to look at these not as waves in the water with their crests projecting up into the air and their troughs low down, but as waves in the air (i.e. waves in the under surface of the air which lies above the water), with their crests projecting downwards into the water and their troughs high up? This may seem odd at first, but we can make ourselves think of waves in that way, and it is in the end as easy one way as the other. If you draw a wavy line on a piece of paper, you can see it either as a series of waves with their crests upwards and their troughs low down, or the other way round, and the same applies to the waves of the sea. They are not *really* the one

only, or *really* the other only. They are both, and
the way we see them depends on which way we
group together for our attention what we are looking at.

Just as in the case of 'selecting', we overlook
the fact that this 'grouping' process is taking place,
because on the whole for practical purposes we all
group together in the same way except in detail.
It is only when we discover that we are 'grouping'
in ways different from those of our neighbours that
we realize that we have been grouping at all.

Let us take another example. Consider the room
you are in, and think of all the objects in it, the
furniture, the desks and tables and cupboards. Think
of these as being the main things in the room, and
regard the air merely as what fills up the space where
there does not happen to be any furniture. This is
what you normally do. On the other hand you could,
if you wished, regard the air as the main thing in the
room, with the furniture merely as what fills up the
space where there happens to be no air. It may seem
odd to think of room and furniture and air in this
way, but you could do so. As a matter of fact, it is
not so very odd. After all, it is the way in which a
health inspector would think of the room if he came
to measure in cubic feet the air space of the room.
He would not merely take measurements of the walls
of the room and calculate upon them only. He
would deduct all the space taken up by cupboards
and so forth, in order to find more exactly how much
air space there was. We do not naturally think of a
room in this way, but with a certain effort of imagination we could do so if required.

Now let us take an example concerning time
rather than space. Think of the swing of a golf club.
Suppose that we watch a good golfer giving a demon-
stration. He walks out to the tee, and takes up his
stance. He grounds his club just behind the ball;

he swings slowly back; he makes a barely perceptible pause at the top of the swing; then he brings the club down, strikes the ball, follows through and ends the swing, and after he has seen where the ball has landed, he lowers his club, and walks off. Then we fall to discussing his swing, commenting critically on this part of it or that. We say, for instance, that his swing back was too slow, or that his follow-through was jerky, or something of the sort.

We all naturally regard the swing as a process that in some way forms a unit by itself. The various stages of it ' belong together '. It would never occur to us to regard the man's walking up to the tee, his grounding of his club and his swing back, as belonging together to form one process; and then to regard his swing down, follow-through and walking away from the tee as another and separate process. With some effort of imagination, we could no doubt regard them in that way if required, though it is not natural to us to do so.

Take another example of ' grouping together ' in time. Again, it seems natural to us that an historian should write a history of the Norman Conquest, beginning with the situation in Normandy and in England in the first half of the eleventh century, and then passing on to the invasion itself and to the Battle of Hastings, and finally to the settling-down process in the latter half of the eleventh century. Many historians have in fact done this. The Conquest seems to form a natural ' historical period '. It would strike us as very odd if an historian were to write a history of the Normans, describing the activities of Duke William and his men up to some point in the middle of the Battle of Hastings on that day in 1066, and stopping there. It would similarly seem very odd if another historian were to write another history beginning in the middle of the Battle of Hastings and stopping in, say, 1091. These would not seem natural 'historical periods'. It is so habitual to us to think of the Norman Conquest, the whole Norman Conquest, as belonging together to form one historical process or period, which is why we give it its own special name, that we overlook the fact that this is only one way of 'grouping together' those events in our attention, and that there are alternative ways of grouping together the same events. These alternative ways may be less satisfactory, but they are equally possible.

We have taken two examples of grouping in space, and two of grouping in time. There is one other principal kind of 'grouping' of which we ought to take an example, namely the grouping together in attention of cause and effect. Has it ever struck you how very remarkable is our way of regarding causes and effects? Think what happened when last you switched on your wireless set. You pressed or turned the switch, and a moment or two later the set started to work and the programme was heard from the loud speaker. It seems obvious that turning the switch caused the wireless set to start working. We think of the turning of the switch and the coming of the sound as 'cause and effect'. They form a pair that seem naturally to go together.

Yet, think how remarkable this is. Your turning of the switch was not the only event that occurred at that instant. All sorts of other events occurred at the same time. Your arm moved, your body moved, your heart beat, somebody in the next room moved, the clock ticked, traffic passed in the street, perhaps the wind rattled the window, and so forth. Innumerable other events of which you were aware happened at that instant, to say nothing of all the other events at that instant of which you were not aware.

Similarly, when a moment or two later the set began to work, that event (the programme making itself heard) was not the only event that occurred.

97

Again there were other events, near you and far away from you, which all happened at that instant. In other words, at one moment an enormous complex of events took place, one among which was the turning of the switch; and a moment later another enormous complex of events took place, one among which was the set's beginning to work and making the programme audible. Out of all this we pick these two events, namely the turning of the switch and the set's beginning to work, and we think of them as a pair that are connected. We 'group them together in our attention', and think of them as 'cause and effect'.

If you ruminate over any instance of causal relationship, you will see that you are picking out and grouping together in your attention two events (or circumstances, or whatever you care to call them), and you are thinking of them as 'belonging together', while you do not think of all the other events that are happening at the same time as 'belonging together' in that same close way. You no doubt have good reason for thinking of each particular pair as 'belonging together', possibly because they always happened together in the past, or for some such reason. The point I am using the examples to emphasize is that we are in this way 'selecting' and 'grouping together' in our attention every moment of the day.

In the case of the wireless set and its switch, the two events that 'belong together' stand out clearly to our view, when once they have been pointed out to us or have been discovered by us for ourselves. Until this is done, they do not stand out in our attention. The primitive tribesmen mentioned in chapter I who do not believe in an inevitable succession of the seasons, did not pick out and group together in their attention the spring season and the summer season, as we do. A substantial part of the work of enlarging human knowledge consists in detecting these pairs of events that go together to form ' cause and effect '.

Again, as in the case of ' selecting ', it would be disproportionate to attempt here to catalogue the different ways in which we ' group together '. I am using these examples mainly to emphasize that this ' grouping together ' does in fact take place, or rather that it has already taken place without our being aware of it, for it is only because that grouping has taken place that the world we experience appears to us as it does. If we ' grouped ' things differently, i.e. if we thought of them as forming different groups, then the world we experience would be different.

At this point the same question will have arisen in your mind as arose about selecting. Why do we group in one way rather than another? What criterion, or principle, or canon do we have? And if I group in one way, and you group in another, is one of us right and the other wrong; or, less extremely, is one way better than the other, and if so, which? This is the topic of the following chapter.

What I have been trying to make clear in this chapter is that the world around us as we experience it, is not just simply ' there ' as we experience it. It is, in a certain colloquial sense of the phrase, very largely ' made by us ', because what we experience is not simply what our sense-organs react to, but is a selection grouped together in certain very remarkable and, within limits, fluctuating ways.

It will be perhaps as well to end this chapter by repeating, in the fuller light of what has emerged in the course of it, a point made at its beginning. We have been dealing with the working of the sense-organs, and with ' selecting ' and ' grouping ', and have naturally discussed first the one, then the second, and then the third. This does not mean that they happen in order, first one and then the second and then the third. They are not separate processes happening one after the other in time. We are compelled to discuss them in this succession, because the limitations of human speech and writing will not let us talk about them all three at once. Further, we are not aware of, and never can be aware of, carrying them out as conscious processes. What we are aware of is the world around us and ourselves in it. We are not aware of the processes that have gone to giving us this knowledge of the world and of ourselves. The only way we can become aware of these processes is the way described in the earlier part of this chapter and called by Kant, in his peculiar terminology, the Transcendental Deduction of the Categories. In less alarming words, this amounts to saying that when we think the matter over, we can see that *something like* these processes, something that can not unfairly be *described as* these processes, must have taken place, in order that the world around us should appear to us as it does. If these processes had been different, then the world would have appeared different to us—as it does appear different to people whose processes are different. We cannot examine these processes directly. We cannot even say from direct inspection that they occur at all. We can only say that, in order that our knowledge should be what we experience it to be, then something more or less like what I have called ' selecting ' and ' grouping ' must have taken place.

CHAPTER IX
What is Truth?

No w let us deal directly with that question which has been obtruding itself at intervals throughout the preceding chapter, namely what is the principle, or criterion, or standard, in accordance with which we adopt one way of 'selecting' and one way of 'grouping' rather than another. This is a highly important question, for it amounts to asking 'What is truth?'

There is a possible confusion to guard against here. This question does not mean 'What is the truth about the ultimate nature of the universe?' If it did, there would be no possible answer, for a reason which will emerge later in this chapter when we are dealing with explanation. By 'What is truth?' I mean 'Wherein does a true statement differ from a false one?' This is a less wildly arrogant question to ask, and there is some prospect of finding an intelligible answer.

The representationist philosophers had been in a position to give a comparatively simple answer. On their view, each of us has inside his mind his own mental representation or picture, while outside is the real world. A man's representation is 'true' if it is a good copy of the real world outside, i.e. if it corresponds to it. A man's representation is 'false' if it does not correspond. So for them, the question of what constitutes the difference between truth and falsity was indeed comparatively simple. On their theory, truth consists in the correspondence of a man's mental representations, or of those representations stated in words, to the outer reality. This theory of theirs was in consequence called the 'correspondence' theory of truth. As you can see, it is a consequence of the representative or 'three term' theory of knowledge, so that people who hold the one theory hold the other also, whether they are aware of doing so or not. If you have agreed with me in abandoning the ' representative ' theory of knowledge, then we must also abandon the 'correspondence' theory of truth. What alternative can we find?

This is not an easy quest. It is much more difficult for us to explain the difference between truth and falsity than it was for philosophers like Locke, because the theory of knowledge which we are now working on is radically unlike theirs. This plunges us into a very involved discussion. I think the best way to deal with it will be to start by considering some examples. To begin with, take as an example some very general and abstract statement, and examine wherein its truth or falsity appears to consist. Consider the truth or falsity of the statement that there is a dependable regularity in natural happenings, i.e. that there are laws of nature which are always fulfilled. Suppose that you become involved in an argument on this subject with somebody who maintains the opposite. This is not an altogether fanciful supposition, for there are now alive large numbers of human beings who, like the primitive tribesmen of chapter I, think that there is no such dependable regularity. You are not very likely to discuss this topic with a primitive tribesman, but you may very well get into an argument with some 'particularly sceptical friend, who maintains that those primitive tribesmen are logically right, and that there is indeed no ground for believing in any such dependable regularity. I expect that you, like me, would say that your sceptical friend was wrong. On what principle are you deciding that your view is sounder than his? What makes you say that the one view is true, and that the other is not true?

What in fact would you do about it, if you were actually to become involved in such an argument?

How would you argue with a man who maintained that there is no logical ground for believing that the vegetation you see around you will in due course change, and that the days will lengthen and shorten in the familiar succession throughout the coming year? It would be no use saying to him : ' Oh well, it has always happened in the past.' He would reply : ' No. In the first place, we don't know that it has always happened in the past. We only know that it has happened in the past so far as the memory and records of man go, including the records deduced by the scientists.' While you were digesting this, he would add : ' And in the second place, no amount of regularity in the past is any logical ground for expecting regularity in the future.' You would find that this point required some consideration. At first you would probably say he was wrong; but then, after thinking it over, you would realize with momentary exasperation that the man was right. You would have to agree that no amount of regularity in the past is any logical ground for expecting regularity in the future, *unless* you already assume a continuing regularity in nature, which is precisely the point in dispute. You would probably pause for a moment, and then return to the attack with the explanation that the earth moved in an approximately elliptic orbit round the sun, and that it rotated diurnally on an axis which was not exactly at right angles to the plane of that orbit, and that this was the cause of the seasonal changes, which therefore came with dependable regularity. This explanation, however, would be no use either, because he would reply that you were not in fact explaining at all, but were merely repeating your first assertion over again in other words, because you were assuming that the earth's axis would *remain* regularly and dependably inclined to its orbit, and that the earth would *continue* to move round the sun in that orbit as before, which is precisely the point at issue; and in saying this he would be fully justified.

If he persisted, you would in the end find yourself driven in exasperation to say something like the following to him : ' Well, if you want to think of the universe as one in which there is no regularity in natural happenings, go away and do so. But—and this is the point—look what happens to you if you do. The result will be that you land yourself in hopeless confusion. If you behave in accordance with the view you are stating (and are not merely saying it in order to be argumentative) then you will not eat a meal, because you have no reason for expecting that it will give you strength and keep you alive. If you do not believe in the dependability of natural laws, then you must believe that anything or nothing might be the consequence of eating a meal. You will not even sit down on a chair, because you have no reason for expecting that it will hold you up. On your view, anything or nothing might be the consequence of sitting down on a chair.'

This conclusion can be stated in general terms. A man can think of the universe as one in which there are no dependable natural laws—if he likes; but if he does so, the consequence is that he confuses himself so thoroughly that he does not know what to do next in the ordinary practical affairs of daily life.

This gives us some guidance in our search for an answer to the question ' What is truth?'

When we are discussing the truth or otherwise of the statement that there are dependable natural laws, we cannot simply inspect the universe and say : ' There are laws of nature ' or ' There are not laws of nature '. By such assertion and counter-assertion we can never reach any conclusion. We can however say : ' Look at the consequences of thinking that there are laws of nature, and look at the consequences of thinking that there are not. The consequences of thinking, or unconsciously assuming, that there are not such natural laws is confusion.' That is to say, if you 'select' and 'group' in accordance with the view that there is a dependable regularity in natural happenings, then the world you experience will be relatively simple and orderly. If on the other hand you 'select' and 'group' in accordance with the view that there is no such dependable regularity, then the world you experience will be one of unmanageable muddle and confusion.

This suggests a perhaps surprising answer to the question 'What is truth?' or 'What is the criterion of truth?' It now begins to look as if the principle on which we decide that one way of 'selecting' and 'grouping' is better than another is one of order and comparative simplicity, taking all the relevant circumstances into account. It looks as if the 'best way', the 'true way', the 'way that gives us truth', is the way that gives us the highest attainable degree of order and simplicity in the world we 'make' for ourselves by our selecting and grouping. It looks as if the truest of the innumerable possible ways in which we 'select' and 'group' in our attention those small scraps of the universe to which our sense-organs react, is the way that makes those scraps fit together in the most orderly and simple way, in the way that makes them 'cohere' best.

This is perhaps easier to see if we take an example from a science. When Einstein was examining the Newtonian physical theories, he found that they explained the phenomena very well, except for some apparently small points which did not fit into the pattern at all. It was known, for instance, that the movements of the planet Mercury were incompatible with the Newtonian physics, as was referred to in another connection on page 66, and there were various other similar cases. This meant that there was something wrong somewhere with the Newtonian way of regarding the physical universe. So Einstein tried first one way and then another, until he found a way of regarding the physical universe, such that the movements of Mercury and also the other hitherto anomalous phenomena did cohere in a comparatively simple and orderly fashion with all the rest of the observations of the astronomers. The view he came to in the end, namely the Einsteinian relativity physics, is no doubt surprising to the layman, but it does enable all the observed facts to fit together into a comparatively simple and orderly whole. This is why the scientists accept it, and this is why they would say, if you asked them, that it is 'true', or at any rate 'truer' than Newton's view. Indeed, it was the insistence of scientists upon simplicity that led to notice being taken of the anomalies, and to the discovery of a solution for them.

There is one point in the above procedure that requires special attention, because it is so typical an instance. Einstein's physics is certainly not more simple and coherent than is Newton's physics, *if Newton's physics is considered by itself*. It is notoriously not so. But it is more simple and coherent than *Newton's physics considered together with the vagaries of Mercury*. The complex situation formed by the Newtonian physics *together with* these more recently discovered irregular movements of Mercury (known to us, but not known in Newton's time) is anything but simple and coherent. Compared with this disorderly complex, the Einsteinian physics is indeed more simple and coherent.

So in this example of the criterion of truth, an example of the criterion by which one abstruse scientific hypothesis is adjudged better than another, it again looks as if the alternative which we consider most true is the one that enables us to regard the relevant situation (using that phrase in the comprehensive sense indicated in the preceding paragraph) in the most simple and orderly way, in the most coherent way. The difference between the true and the false seems to be turning out to be the difference between what is comparatively more and what is comparatively less effective in enabling us to 'select' and 'group' in a simple, orderly, and coherent way. This view of the nature of truth, in terms of which these two examples have been interpreted, is radically different from the older 'correspondence' theory. In contra-distinction, it is commonly called the 'coherence' theory of truth.

At first, I expect you feel that this new account of truth seems sound enough. But now a doubt will occur to you. This account of the nature of truth and falsity may be adequate as regards highly general statements or abstruse scientific hypotheses, such as the two examples quoted; but, you may well ask, is it a sound account of the difference between truth and falsity in the case of a plain, blunt statement of fact ? If you consider the statement : ' This pipe cost five shillings ', then it certainly looks as if this statement were either just true or just false, and that the question of coherence and comparative simplicity had nothing to do with it.

There must be something wrong here. This theory of the nature of truth and falsity must either hold of all kinds of statements, or else it is an inadequate theory and ought not to be accepted. Later in this inquiry, I think you will come to see that in spite of appearances, such plain, blunt statements of fact are exactly like very general statements and scientific hypotheses as regards the criterion of their truth. The same theory of truth does explain them all, but before we can hope to see this, we need to make an excursion from the main line of the argument into the question of language and meaning. This, however, is by no means a wasteful diversion of interest, as the excursion is well worth undertaking for its own sake.

Consider the matter in this way. Why should we come to think, as in the second last paragraph we did find ourselves thinking, that plain statements of fact are somehow different in nature from very general statements and scientific hypotheses? If we can see how this has come about, the whole situation will become clearer. The cause seems to be as follows. In the cases of the very general statement and the scientific hypothesis, we did not think of ourselves as examining the truth or otherwise of a statement *considered by itself as a statement*. We thought of ourselves as being concerned with the truth or otherwise of a view or hypothesis which I or you, or at any rate somebody, holds about the matter under discussion. What we were discussing was whether the way I look at things, or you, or the sceptical friend, or Newton, or Einstein, was satisfactory or not. It was therefore natural for us to regard the question as one of whether the way of ' selecting ' and ' grouping ' taken by me, or you, or whoever it might be, was a satisfactory way or not.

On the other hand, when we were considering the truth or otherwise of: ' This pipe cost five shillings ', we did not at first think of ourselves as discussing anybody's way of looking at things. Instead, we thought we were discussing the truth or otherwise of a plain statement which existed by itself, and had to be either true or false, whether or not anybody at all expressly uttered it, or even thought it. It is this difference that gives plain statements of fact the appearance of being somehow different from general statements and scientific hypotheses.

The question therefore is whether we were right or wrong in thinking that there is such a difference. In the case of a plain statement of fact, are we discussing a statement by itself, or are we really discussing the way in which somebody looks at things, just as we are in the case of a very general statement or an abstruse scientific hypothesis? This is the crux of the matter. The answer to this question, as it appears to me (though some other philosophers, remember, would disagree), is that in such a case we are not discussing a statement by itself, but are in fact discussing the way somebody looks at things, in the same way as we were in the cases of very general views and abstruse scientific hypotheses, and are employing the same criterion of truth.

If this is so, why should the contrary be so naturally taken for granted by us, as it clearly is until we make some special inquiry? There is an explanation, and this is where the topic of language comes in, for the explanation lies in an assumption we have all unconsciously made about the nature of language and meaning.

This fundamental assumption which we all make, in our unsophisticated days, about the nature of language is that in some way the words and sentences contain their meaning within themselves. By primitive peoples, this assumption is made with an often remarkable matter-of-factness. In many primitive communities there is a taboo on mentioning a man's name except in certain special circumstances, because his name is believed to contain within it something of himself, which would be dissipated if his name were uttered except under special precautions. A similar belief that words are somehow real things containing a meaning and influence within themselves underlies those old fairy tales in which a princess inadvertently transforms herself into an animal by repeating the efficacious words of a magic spell without even knowing what they mean. Some theologians hold that a similar belief, on a higher plane and in an attenuated form, is involved in some, though certainly not in all, of the Christian dogmas about 'the Word' in the Gospel of St John.

This belief about words is widely spread. Among the more primitive and the uneducated it is universal. A remarkably matter-of-fact practical application of it occurs even at the present day in the Tibetan prayer-wheel. If, thinks the Tibetan peasant, a prayer uttered once does some good, then the same prayer uttered many times will do more good. Therefore, since he assumes that the efficacy lies in the prayer as an entity in itself, he writes it round the rim of a wheel, and then frugally employs the water of a mountain stream to turn it all day long, instead of wastefully employing his own lungs and lips to enunciate it.

By less primitive peoples, such as ourselves, this same assumption about the nature of language is still made, with or without a recognition of it. We have all felt, on completing some long and informative letter, that we have packed our meaning into those words and sentences on those particular sheets of paper. As we post the letter, we look at it, bulging with its many sheets, and we have the satisfying feeling that it is stuffed full of news and meaning. Sometimes we are aware that this is no more than a feeling, sometimes not.

By other people, usually regarded as at the other extreme of subtle sophistication in such matters, namely formal logicians, this assumption is also made, and again with or without a recognition of its having been made. The traditional formal logic, commonly called simply 'logic', and its modern derivatives are unintelligible unless it is assumed that there exist units of meaning, commonly called 'propositions', which are significant in themselves irrespective of anyone's enunciating or even thinking them, just as there exist units of language called sentences. These logicians, though otherwise of course very different from the Tibetan peasant in their modes of thought, yet make a fundamental assumption about the nature of language which is in essentials the same as his.

I believe that these assumptions about the nature of language, so very widely spread and so unquestioningly accepted, are fundamentally wrong and perniciously misleading, but again I must warn the reader that many contemporary philosophers, especially those describing themselves as logicians, would disagree with me.

There is, of course, a very close connection between holding these assumptions about the nature of language and holding the representationist or ' three term ' assumption about the nature of knowledge, of which it is, in fact, one particular exemplification. The working out of the connection is an exercise the reader can undertake for himself. He will see that if the representationist view of the nature of knowledge is abandoned, then the foregoing assumptions about the nature of language must be abandoned also. In practice, however, students of philosophy seldom advance in this way. They usually abandon these two assumptions by separate inquiry, and it is only after they have done so that they discover the connection between them. That was my experience, and the discovery of the connection was a memorable enlightenment.

The reason for the common acceptance of that initial assumption about the nature of language appears to be as follows. The structure of language is extremely complex, but it is on the whole easy to examine. The results of this examination are embodied in the various traditional grammars of the classical and modern languages. We are all more or less familiar from our schooldays with the traditional grammar of at least our own language, and we therefore think of language as the grammarians have led us to do. The essential point on which their traditional grammar insists is that the complex and lengthy discourses in which we normally speak and write are built up by the combination in various ways of fundamental units called sentences, a sentence, according to the traditional grammarians, being a self-complete unit of language which can exist significantly by itself. This we all unconsciously assume, and it is therefore natural that we, like the logicians mentioned above, should equally unconsciously assume the consequence of this, namely, that each sentence contains or carries in some way within it a self-complete unit of meaning. From this it would follow, again quite naturally and reasonably, that these self-complete units of meaning must be either true or false in themselves, independently of any other units of meaning, and without reference to any person who might speak or write or think them. We may disagree with these logicians and others who hold these views, but we can see how natural it is for them to hold them.

If, then, we set out with this initial assumption about the nature of language, and are in consequence involved in assuming that there exist units of meaning which must be either true or false in themselves, then it is not at all surprising that we should think that the question of the truth or falsity of plain statements such as 'This pipe cost five shillings' is one of the truth or falsity of that statement considered as a statement or unit of meaning by itself, and that it is not a question of the comparative simplicity and order of any particular person's way of 'selecting' and 'grouping'. This is why at first it appears to us that plain statements of fact are different in kind from very general statements and scientific hypotheses, and that they have a different criterion of truth.

So far, so good. But now the more obviously

interesting question arises, whether this initial assumption about the nature of language is justified. It turns out not to be so. Speech is not a series of symbols somehow carrying meaning within them, as the Tibetan thinks his prayer on his wheel carries its meaning within it. Speech is simply gesture made audible. Speech is simply gesture that can be listened to, instead of watched. Speech is an extremely complex system of more or less standardized and conventionalized noises, and writing is an even more highly standardized and conventionalized system of visible marks upon a surface, but, in principle, speech and writing are as much gesture as is pointing with the finger.

The origin of language appears to have been roughly as follows. Our remotest human ancestors, when they attempted to draw the attention of others of their kind to anything in particular (or when they behaved in a way which did in fact draw attention to it, intention or no intention) pointed and gesticulated in its direction. These movements were accompanied by various movements in the flexible tissues in other parts of the body, especially when any high degree of vigour was put into the action. Among these were movements in the tongue, lips, windpipe and associated parts. This was further accompanied in certain cases by contraction of the walls of the chest and movements of the diaphragm, which led to the expulsion of air from the lungs through the windpipe over the tongue and between the teeth and lips, thereby creating noises. The gestures and the noises together resulted in drawing attention to the object or situation in question, and then in course of time the noises alone served to do so, i.e. the noises became significant speech. Later, after thousands upon thousands of years, conventionalized marks upon surfaces came to be employed to represent the conventionalized noises.

Consider an example. When a biologist writes, and you read, that the hind leg of a horse is homologous with your own leg (i.e. that it is similar in structure, though it may look different because the proportions are different), what is happening? What he does is to arrange the printer's black marks on paper so cunningly that you, sitting in your chair by the fire, have your attention drawn to certain matters to which he could otherwise have drawn your attention only by leading you up to a horse and pointing with his hands. If he had used his hands alone, he could by pointing have made you notice that your leg and the horse's hind leg appeared altogether different, because your leg is jointed in the middle, so that the lower part below the knee can bend backwards but not forwards, while the horse's hind leg is jointed in the middle so that the lower part can bend forwards but not backwards. The biologist could then by gesture make you bend your knee, raising your heel but keeping the ball of your foot on the ground, and he could point to the horse's middle joint and to your ankle (not your knee). It would then begin to dawn on you that these two did in some way correspond. He could next point to your knee and to the horse's large upper joint encased in the flesh of its haunch, and you would then see clearly that these corresponded also, and that your leg and the horse's hind leg were indeed homologous. Whether he points with his hands or uses black marks printed in a book is only a difference of technique. It is in practice a very important difference, because much more subtle matters can in many cases be pointed out by words and sentences than can be pointed out by the hands; but whichever technique he adopts, what he is doing is in principle the same. By pointing or by words he is making you select for attention the bone structure of the horse's leg and of your own, and is making you neglect the remainder of what your sense-organs are capable of detecting in the situation, and he is making you group together what you select in such a way that the horse's leg and your own no longer appear merely different, but are seen as essentially similar in structure, even though they differ in the relative proportions of their parts. In exactly the same sort of way, what I am doing in writing this book consists in directing the printer to make certain series of conventional black marks upon a much-folded area of paper, these being arranged in the best way I can think of to draw your attention to certain states of affairs, including your own mental processes, and to make you select for attention certain parts or aspects thereof, in such a way that the whole of your relevant experience will fit together or cohere into a relatively simple and orderly whole. In exactly the same sort of way, Einstein, in the example concerning Mercury, used written German and mathematical symbols, both of extreme complexity, in order to make physicists ' select ' and ' group ' to form a relatively simple and coherent whole.

If the biologist in our example were unskilful in pointing, you might have difficulty in understanding what he was driving at when he pointed. To be effective, he needs some natural aptitude and a good deal of acquired skill gained by long practice. If he were unskilful in handling the English language, you might similarly have difficulty in understanding what he was driving at when he wrote. Here also to be effective he needs both some natural aptitude and a good deal of acquired skill gained by long practice.

Whether or not a writer succeeds in his purpose depends on a number of considerations. In the case of this book, for instance, whether or not I succeed depends partly on whether the way of ' selecting ' and ' grouping ' of which I am thinking does in fact produce a relatively simple and orderly whole;

partly on whether you make the not inconsiderable effort required to understand; and partly on my competence or otherwise in the handling of written English. If I bungle my use of language, I may direct your attention to the wrong things or in the wrong way, or may leave you in doubt as to what it is that I am trying to direct your attention to.

Discovering what is best to direct your attention to is the work of the biologist or physicist or philosopher, as such. To use written English or other language to carry out the directing is the art of the literary craftsman, and there is no necessary connection between the two. The two kinds of work have to be laboured on separately, though each does react upon the other to some extent. Men who are good at the one are not necessarily good at the other, and men who enjoy the one do not necessarily enjoy the other, and may even find it distasteful. The naturally easy expositor is seldom given to original thinking; and the original thinker is irritated by the detailed work of exposition, unless he has something of the artist in him and enjoys exposition as a work of art. Plato did so, as his Dialogues show, but it is a melancholy commonplace that most of the greater philosophers, as for instance Kant, did not so enjoy exposition, with the result that their books are extremely difficult to read. This is of course partly due to the difficulty of the subject, but it is also due to the fact that the books in question were printed from manuscripts which were still in the form of notes for a book, rather than in the form in which a completed book ought to be. They were published in that form because life is short. Their authors not unnaturally preferred to spend the available time in going on with further inquiries, rather than in the arduous and frequently exasperating work of labouring upon the written language, recasting it, and again recasting it, until a form of verbal gesture, which is what language is, was reached which would draw the competent reader's attention to what was required and to nothing else. These difficulties apply even to an introductory book such as this. You have, I hope, been finding this book tolerably simple and easy to read and follow. At least I hope you are aware of being led on from point to point in something that feels like a congenial succession of development. This has come about, in so far as it has come about at all, only because what you are now reading is the last of many drafts. Had you been faced with the earlier drafts, you would have found them very difficult to follow. The best way to improve one's writing is to get a larger wastepaper basket.

Now let us return to our biologist. The drawing of your attention to the homology between the horse's leg and your own leg would probably not be the only result of his pointing. You might well find that he had started you thinking not only of horses' legs, but of riding a horse at the gallop and hearing and feeling the wind past your ears and the beat of the hooves on the turf, which is what is happening to me as I write about it, or he might have started you thinking of some childhood holiday spent on a farm, or of some other 'associations', as we commonly call them. Further, all sorts of feelings and emotions might be aroused in you, according as you are interested or not in horses and their legs.

If you were reading the biologist's book, precisely the same would occur. The words and sentences would not only direct your attention to the homology, but would also direct your attention to these associated matters, and they would also arouse these emotions and feelings. This parallelism between pointing and the use of words is interestingly complete, if you work it out. The biologist could not have pointed out the horse's joints unless he had possessed hands. If he had not suitable and manageable hands and fingers with which to point, then we should either not understand him at all, or should misunderstand him. Similarly in his book, if he had not suitable and manageable words to write with we should either not understand him at all, or should misunderstand him. For some purposes there are suitable words available in our vocabularies. For others there are not. Since men through countless' generations have conventionalized and developed this system of symbolic pointing which we call language, we can all generally find suitable words to direct other people's attention to what we wish, provided that it is the commonplace things of daily life that we wish to direct their attention to. On the other hand, when we wish to direct their attention, and our own, to less plain and obvious matters, we fall into difficulty, because we have to use for that purpose words which were originally developed and used for other and more matter-of-fact purposes, i.e. we have to use words as metaphors. The parallelism between having words to write with and fingers to point with is very close.

Again, if this biologist had singularly beautiful hands and moved them gracefully, you might find your attention concentrated on them, rather than on what they were pointing to. You might find greater interest and pleasure in the beauty of their form and the grace of their movement than in the homology between your leg and the horse's leg. In the same way, if he were to write singularly beautiful English prose, you might find enjoyment and interest rather in the ring and rhythm of his words and sentences than in the things he was using those words and sentences to point out.

In the case of a biological text-book, and in similar writings, the grace and rhythm of the word pattern are comparatively irrelevant, as are any emotions that might be aroused, or any associations that might be revivified. The writer on such subjects must of course write English that is not unduly disjointed or cacophonous, and he must avoid arousing ludicrous associations and unwelcome emotions, but beyond this, he is not greatly concerned with such points. On the other hand, in those writings commonly called 'literary', the situation is different in some respects. Think of any familiar verse of poetry or passage of prose that gives you delight, and analyse your enjoyment of it. You will find that only a part of the enjoyment comes from the contemplation of the situation to which it draws your attention. Much comes from the beauty of the words, considered as a mere pattern of sound and rhythm; and from the emotions it arouses in you; and from the associated situations it happens also to make you think of.

You will notice that the distinction between 'scientific' and 'emotive' language which is nowadays in process of percolating from philosophic discussion into common usage, is not, as it is frequently taken to be, a distinction between two radically different kinds of language, or two radically different purposes for which language is used. The distinction is between instances of the relative predominance in the one case of the emotion-arousing purpose or effect of language, and in the other case of the simple 'pointing out' purpose or effect.

(These preliminary considerations on the relative predominance or absence of the various factors in the purposes and effects of language make a topic for you to ruminate on at leisure and to follow up for yourself. If you do this you will find that you are working out a fairly comprehensive theory of literary criticism, which you can further extend to include music and the plastic arts.)

Now let us see how this excursion into the

origins and nature of language bears upon our inquiry into the nature of truth. On pointing out the homology between your leg and a horse's hind leg, the biologist needs to use some words as metaphors, but only a few, as you would see by going over the discussion again. But when we attempt to describe the ways in which we know and learn and explain, we have to use metaphors throughout. We ' increase our knowledge '. We ' deepen our understanding '. We have ' more knowledge ' or ' less knowledge '. We speak of ' spreading a rumour ', and of ' collecting information ', and the like. These metaphors are most convenient verbal devices, and are indeed the only reasonably brief verbal devices for the purpose that we have, and the use of them is a most convenient practice. The only alternatives are either to invent completely new words (which is what some philosophers have been driven to do in despair at the misunderstanding consequent upon overlooking the fact that these metaphors are only metaphors), or else to put up with very long descriptive periphrases, which is what you and I have mostly had to do in the discussions in this book.

Much misunderstanding of the nature of knowledge has come from overlooking the fact that these metaphors are only metaphors. Many of the very unsatisfactory teaching methods, for instance, which are so serious a practical handicap in many parts of our educational system, are based on the failure to recognize that our common habit of speaking of knowledge as an entity that can be spread or transmitted from one mind to another is only a metaphor. Of course, as so often happens in such cases, these teaching methods, e.g. those of the instructor sergeant who expects his men to know by rote the details of a given drill, or those of the professor of anatomy who conducts his class on similar lines, are not just perversely silly If knowledge really were what they think it is, then their teaching methods would be very sound. Unfortunately, practitioners of such methods are seldom given to abstract thought, and it has never occurred to them that their practice is based on a general theory of knowledge, and that this theory may be wrong. This is why it is so difficult to persuade them to change their methods, as this would require them first to recognize that they are applying a certain theory of knowledge, then to examine and abandon it, and then to adopt a better one in its place, all of which require an unusually open and agile mind. (Note that these two adjectives are themselves metaphorical.)

Contrary to what we are led by misuse of metaphors to believe, knowledge is not something that can be accumulated in a mind which would otherwise be blank or empty. We do not begin in sheer ignorance. The technique of successful education would be much simpler if we did. We begin in *mis*understanding. We begin by 'selecting' and 'grouping' in scrappy and unintegrated ways. There is an historical explanation for these ways, either in our personal histories or in the history of the race, and they have become congenial to us by long habituation. To increase our knowledge, as we say, is not to place something where there was nothing before. To increase our knowledge is to alter for the better our ways of 'selecting' and 'grouping'; to notice what we did not notice before; and to notice it in ways which are new to us, and probably strange.

The difference between the educated and the uneducated is not only that the educated are aware of, and respond to, more of the complex reality about us than the uneducated. This they undoubtedly do, and have richer interests accordingly, but this is a lesser difference. The principal difference is that the educated see what they experience as fitting together systematically into a pattern which, while adequate, is reasonably simple and coherent, whereas the uneducated do not. The views of the uneducated on one subject remain uncorrelated with their views on others, thereby bringing confusion into their judgements and decisions on practical affairs, without their having any notion of this incoherence. It is much easier and more comfortable—in the short run—to leave our views on one subject uncorrelated with our views on others. This is why the process of being educated is a strenuous one, and why there is in all of us a certain natural resistance to the process, which we have to overcome by our own effort, assisted no doubt in our younger days by a certain amount of pressure from teachers and professors, and by the jolts of experience.

The difficulties of teaching are not therefore due to some special and ingenious perversity of mind in the pupil, as teachers in exasperation are sometimes tempted to believe, but are natural and inevitable difficulties, with which a sound educational method ought to be able to deal as a matter of course. The method which is traditional in our present educational system is the indirect one of making the pupil study the various subjects of his curriculum not only for their own sakes, but also for the effect such study has in developing the capacity for integrating the previously unintegrated, independently of the value of the subjects in themselves. In this lies the element of truth in the old dictum that you can educate a man for modern life by bringing him up on the classics. Unfortunately, though there is this element in the effects of a classical education alone, there are other elements also, which are less adequate as an equipment with which to understand the modern world. It may in the future be possible to work out some less indirect methods of producing, or assisting to produce, an educated mind. This book, by the way, is a tentative experiment in that direction.

Contrary to what we are led by misuse of metaphors to believe, knowledge is not an entity that can be transmitted from one mind to others. Indeed, even to speak of 'knowledge' is to use a metaphor. There is not, except in metaphor, any 'common stock of knowledge' in which we share. There are only persons—you, and me, and the next man—who 'select' and 'group', each in his own way and each for himself, certain small parts of the complex mass of influences that surround us; while by the use of language or of any of the accepted system of symbols (e.g. algebraic symbols and the like), we can make each other select for attention certain parts which we should not otherwise have selected, and group them together in ways in which we should not otherwise have grouped them. What we call traditions, myths, 'stocks of knowledge', 'the accumulated insight of the race', and the like, which we speak of as handed down from generation to generation, are *ways* in which we, the separate individuals, 'select' and 'group' in our attention, and correspondingly act.

Take an example. When we are thinking of any subject, say geology, we must not think that there exists any stock of geological knowledge accumulated by geologists in the past and present, of which we get such share as we can. A sounder view of the situation is rather to think that there exists this fragment of the universe that we call the earth, and the rocks and waters upon its outer crust, and that there are many individual geologists who noticed certain fragments of that complex situation, and grouped together what they noticed in certain ways. What we call 'learning geology' is simply coming to select for attention the things the geologists selected, and to group them together in our attention as the geologists grouped them.

When, therefore, we are discussing the truth or otherwise of the plainest and most factual statement as well as of the most abstruse theory, what we are really discussing is the adequacy or otherwise of a view which some person holds of some parts or aspects of the universe. We are really discussing whether the way in which somebody 'selects' and 'groups' is a comparatively simple and coherent way, or is not.

So when we are discussing the truth or otherwise of the plain, blunt statement 'This pipe cost five shillings', what we are in effect doing is to ask : 'If I view the relevant situation on the assumption that this pipe cost five shillings, then does my relevant experience fit together into a reasonably simple and orderly whole? Does it "cohere"? Does it, in less technical language, "make sense"?' That is to say, if you 'select' and 'group' what you saw and read and did about buying this pipe and what you say about its price as being five shillings, does it all fit together into a pattern or whole that is reasonably simple and coherent?

In this case, it does. If on the other hand your statement had been 'This pipe cost seven shillings', then it would not have fitted together. It would be incoherent. Certain parts of it, of course, would cohere among themselves. (The situation is similar to that discussed on page 106.) The fact that you received some change from a ten-shilling note would cohere with a price of seven shillings, but the fact that the shopkeeper said 'five shillings' would not cohere with a price of seven shillings. The only way in which the whole lot can be made to fit together in an orderly and coherent fashion is that the price should be five shillings, which is what we mean, in effect, by saying that the statement is true. We are using the same criterion of truth, the same standard by which to judge ways of 'selecting' and 'grouping', whether we are dealing with very general statements, or with abstruse scientific statements, or with the plainest and most commonplace statements of fact.

At this point you may very reasonably complain of feeling intellectually somewhat breathless, because the effect of the preceding pages, if I have written them competently, will be to make so drastic a change in your outlook on the nature of truth and falsity that you cannot adapt yourself all at once. However, as you ruminate over this change, and grow familiar with it, you will find that it ceases to seem a change at all, and becomes the normal way of regarding the matter. For that reason, this chapter, unlike the earlier and easier ones, will require re-reading. So my advice to you is to read on now, and to return again after an interval to the difficult passages. You will find that after a lapse of time, in which you have been occupied about other matters and have not thought about philosophy at all, these difficult passages will have more or less clarified themselves. In dealing with the understanding of very abstract matters, this is the way our minds seem to work.

Taking this advice, we can now go on to the next natural topic of inquiry. You can see how we are now in a better position to understand the nature of explanation, which is a very puzzling topic when considered by itself. Take some example of a very complex and puzzling situation and of an explanation of it. The Mohammedans and the Jews regard the pig as unclean and will not eat pork. Why should this be so? Our natural first attempt at an explanation is that this must have arisen from experience of the ill effects of eating pork in the hot climates originally inhabited by the Jews and the Mohammedans. This explanation that pork in these hot climates goes bad readily and causes trichinosis and other diseases will however not work, as there appears to be no significant difference between pork and beef or mutton in this respect, and in any case other peoples in the same climates, living in the same towns and villages, eat pork and remain healthy.

To explain this situation, we have to go farther afield and a long way back into the past. This taboo on eating a certain animal is not by any means unique. Many and indeed most primitive peoples of whom we have any knowledge regard certain animals as specifically 'unclean', and treat them with a mixture of fear and awe. It appears that these primitive tribes, and the primitive ancestors of the Mohammedans and the Jews, regarded the animal in question as in some way embodying the spirit or power of the tribe. They hence regarded it as being holy or sacred. Dealings with it by any person other than the priests were therefore considered highly dangerous, both to the tribe and to the interfering person. This belief that holy things are dangerous is ancient and widespread. It is an extremely matter-of-fact and unmystical notion. A divine power is considered to be in some way *in* the holy animal or object, which has in consequence to be kept properly insulated, because if it were touched by the wrong things or persons, this divine power would flow out and be wasted, and would incidentally destroy the thing or person through whom it flowed. This may seem odd to us, but to the primitive it seems common sense, exactly as to us to-day it seems common sense to think that if I were to climb a pylon in the Grampians and touch the electric cables I should not only short-circuit the current, and thus waste the property of the Central Electricity Board, but should also injure and probably kill myself. A very similar belief is sometimes found in connection with primitive kingship. Many primitive tribes, including, I am told, some in Upper Burma to this day, regard their king as embodying within himself the spirit or power of the tribe, and they therefore will not permit him to walk upon the ground for fear that the power or virtue should leak out of him, thus endangering the tribe. He must either be carried, or walk only upon a carpet. The modern custom of putting down a red carpet for the king on formal occasions may well be a survival of that ancient custom and belief.

If you were to ask the men who put down the red carpet what the purpose of it was, they would probably reply that it was intended for the comfort and convenience of the monarch. Yet, from common observation, backed by the comments on Court etiquette recorded of monarchs in the recent past, it appears that such customs are in fact a considerable inconvenience to the monarch. The argument concerning comfort and convenience appears not to be the ground of the custom, but is an attempt to find a contemporary rational explanation for a custom already in existence. It is the custom of customs to survive in practice long after the reason on which they were originally based has been abandoned and forgotten. New reasons are then invented to explain them. The British Constitution is a museum of such survivals, with modern explanations invented to account for them. Such survivals plentifully exist, in the life of individuals and of societies. Much of the texture of daily life is made up of them.

It appears, then, that certain tribes and races regard certain animals as holy because they embody the spirit of the tribe; hence as dangerous for the profane to meddle with; and hence in later times as 'unclean', because the feeling of horror at the thought of eating the sacred animal survives as a feeling long after the originating ground for that feeling has been forgotten. At a very early period, the cultural ancestors of the Mohammedans and the Jews appear to have regarded the pig in this way, and were hence careful to avoid dealings with it, and most particularly to avoid anything so dangerous as eating it.

This gives us an adequate explanation so far, but now there is a difficulty. Some of these primitive tribes eat their sacred animal at certain feasts. What can be the explanation of this apparent extreme contradiction? The explanation appears to be that they consume the animal, in certain specially prepared circumstances, in order to get the power or virtue of it into themselves. This is a very common primitive practice. Cannibals will eat the body of a valiant foe, in order to get his valour, while they will not eat the body of an enemy who died a coward's death, for fear of getting his cowardice into themselves. If the animal embodies the spirit or god of the tribe, then they will in certain circumstances eat it, in order to get the spirit or god into themselves. This ritual eating of a god is very common.

These primitive beliefs and practices may seem absurd to us, but notice that if you grant the fundamental belief on which they are based, namely that there exists a spirit of the tribe, and that it is embodied in an animal or man, then the various taboos and precautions and ritual eatings are just as common-sense and logical as is, say, the spreading of oil upon the surface of stagnant pools in the tropics if you believe that malaria is caused by the bite of the anopheles mosquito which breeds there.

This instance was taken as being a fairly complex example of what happens when we succeed in explaining anything. We began with the puzzling fact that professing Jews and Mohammedans will not eat pork though there appears to be no rational ground why they should deprive themselves of it. Then after some consideration we reached an explanation which enabled us to understand how this restriction had arisen in the remote past and how it had come to survive to-day under such different circumstances. Within our present limits it is an adequate explanation, and it has given us that characteristic feeling of intellectual satisfaction that accompanies the finding of adequate explanations. Now, just what is this process of explanation that has been going on here? When we began, we considered the fact that Jews and Mohammedans will not eat pork as an isolated fact, unrelated or comparatively unrelated to the rest of our knowledge of human nature now and in the past. But we now no longer see this fact as merely isolated and unrelated. Instead, we see it as a part of a wider whole, which considered as a whole is reasonably simple and coherent. Explanation does not consist, as we say in convenient metaphor, in finding ' a reason ' for the puzzling fact or situation. It consists in finding a way of regarding the fact or situation so that it is seen as an integral part of a larger whole or system; that is, it consists in finding a way of ' selecting ' and ' grouping ' such that we are able, so to speak, to stand farther back and see not only the fact or situation by itself in isolation, but the wider situation of which it is a part. In other words, the previously unrelated fact or situation falls into a place in the pattern.

If you take some similar instances of explanation in the sciences, and in the common affairs of everyday life, you will find that the same is the case there too.

This sets the whole question of the nature of explanation in a new light. It shows why no explanation of certain matters is possible. It shows why certain questions cannot be answered and cannot properly be asked. In particular it sets in a new light the question of the ultimate explanation of the universe, which has been so long sought for by so many philosophers, and by us all in exceptionally calm and exceptionally critical periods of our lives. I remember that when I was a boy I often wondered why this mysterious universe (including God as well as His creation) existed at all. You very probably did so also at times. Neither you nor I have ever found any explanation that did not turn out on examination to be bogus, and neither has anybody else. Of course innumerable alleged explanations have been found. Most of these were inspiring, or perhaps merely gratifying, to those who accepted them, but when considered with intellectual honesty as explanations, they all fail, for the very good reason that no such explanation is possible, because the question why this universe exists is meaningless. Explanation of a fact or situation consists in finding a way of regarding it so that it is seen as an integral part of a larger whole or system. We can therefore explain parts of the universe, by relating them to the rest, that is by thinking of them as parts fitting into a wider pattern, but we cannot explain the universe itself, because there is no wider pattern into which to fit it.

In this connection there may arise a devastating misunderstanding against which it is well to guard explicitly. Because no explanation of the universe has been, or can be, found, it is sometimes despairingly concluded that human life is futile and worthless. This does not follow. Such a conclusion is illegitimate. It is also, I believe, frivolous, though this is a topic not strictly in place here. It is, however, very much in place to point out explicitly that the impossibility of any explanation of the universe as a whole is no ground for concluding that human life is worthless, or human effort vain. That impossibility in itself justifies no conclusion, one way or the other. There is equally no justification for the common tendency to argue conversely that because human life is not futile, there must be some explanation for the universe as a whole which would provide an explanation why human life is worth while. Both of these misunderstandings occur frequently in non-learned discussions, and are not unknown in learned discussions also.

The last three chapters have suggested for your consideration an outline of a theory of knowledge, but this still lies throughout under the standing reservation notified at the end of chapter I, on page 19. The whole discussion has proceeded as if we were purely reasoning and contemplative beings. But we are very far from being merely reasoning and contemplative. We have other sides to our natures, and these complexities in human nature have a much closer and more intimate relation to, and effect upon, knowing and the increase of knowledge than is commonly recognized. Any outline of a theory of knowledge must take them into account.

The processes conveniently described as ' selecting and grouping in the relatively simplest and most coherent ways ' do not happen automatically of themselves. They require effort. You will have noticed that the more we go on examining these processes the more they turn out to be active rather than passive. Like everyone brought up by an educational system of which the foundations were laid by men who accepted or assumed a representative theory of knowledge, we used to think that knowing in itself is a passive process. Of course we thought that putting ourselves in the way of gaining more knowledge is an action requiring effort, but knowing itself seemed to us a merely contemplative process. It now turns out to be anything but this. Even the simplest and apparently most inactive kind of experiencing, such as lying idly in the shade listening to the larks singing, in quietly congenial company on a warm afternoon in summer, is not at all a passive process. To select for attention the song of the lark amid the multitudinous variety of other contemporary sounds, and to group the successive sounds of the song together in our attention as belonging together and forming a bird-song, is an active process requiring a certain amount of mental effort.

If we do not make that effort, which in this case is so far within our powers that we do not notice that it is an effort at all, then we should not have that particular experience. We should instead have a different and less integrated experience. Probably, indeed, if we were merely reasoning beings and did not have impulses and emotions and interests to drive us on, we should not have anything worth calling experience at all.

Further, there are emotional and other complexities in the depths of human nature which affect that effort, and the ways in which it is exerted or not exerted. We may not always be inclined, and sometimes not even able, to make the necessary effort. We are men and women with feelings and emotions and impulses and interests (in both senses of ' interest ', i.e. both what arouses our interest and what is to our interest or against it). These complexities of our natures may assist us, or impede us, or even altogether inhibit us in our ways of ' selecting ' and ' grouping '.

If we were mere intellects, we should no doubt ' select ' and ' group ' in the most simple and coherent ways open to us. In other words, we should seek truth disinterestedly. But if we were to do this, we might in many cases cause some distasteful shock to our emotions and feelings, and run counter to our interests. We tend therefore to ' select ' and ' group ' in ways that are simple and coherent—and yet tolerably comfortable. Such situations are often misdescribed as arising from conflict between the reason and the feelings or emotions. This is loose talk. What occurs is better described by saying that in the given situation there are alternative possible ways of selecting and grouping. One way may be markedly more coherent, but may also be disturbing and painful to the feelings and emotions, while the alternative may be noticeably incoherent yet

soothing and satisfying to the feelings and suscepti-
bilities. The truth is not always palatable, and
people of both sexes and all ages tend to notice what
is pleasant and comfortable to notice, and to disregard what is painful and disturbing to face. Accept-
ing the truth when it is unpalatable is congenitally
difficult for most people, and in some cases insuper-
ably so. This applies whether the matter in hand is
great or small, and it also applies whether we know
even vaguely what we are doing or whether we are
totally unconscious of it.

Take an example of a consciously held opinion
on the philosophical scale. There is a very strong
tendency, apparently ineradicable in human nature,
and very powerful unless severely disciplined, to
describe, when philosophizing, not what one finds
the universe to be but what one thinks it ought to
be, what one thinks it must be, in order that it
may accord with one's own highest ideals. There
is said to be an epitaph in a Scottish kirkyard which
runs :

> Here lie I, Martin Elginbrod,
> Have mercy on my soul, Lord God,
> As I would do if I were God,
> And Thou wert Martin Elginbrod.

Many philosophical books have been written by men
who were describing the universe not as they found
it, but as they would have created it had they been
God, that is to say as they desperately hoped it was,
in spite of appearances to the contrary. This type of
writing tells us a certain amount about the writer,
but nothing about the universe, except that it is a
universe which contains such hopes.

The same tendency is shown on a slightly more
restricted level in the muddled thinking about ' high
ideals ' which is so prevalent in political discussion.
If a sanitary engineer draws up a first-class drainage
plan for your house, and sets about getting it installed,

and will not let the contractors fob off anything second-rate upon him, then he has high ideals of a drainage system. If, on the other hand, he tells you that the present drainage system of your house is sound, when in fact it is defective and is infecting your family with typhoid fever, then you do not say that he has high ideals about drainage systems. You say he is incompetent and culpably so, and ought to be dealt with accordingly. Too many politicians have made this same mistake (which can be conveniently called the Martin Elginbrod fallacy) and have thereby brought about in the long run much avoidable human misery by their wilful blindness. A man who sees only good in all things and people is not necessarily exhibiting saintliness. He is more probably exhibiting defective judgement. There may be understandable psychological reasons for this in his disposition or in his past, but it nevertheless is highly culpable if he is in a position of authority, official or personal, so that other people act on his judgement and are led thereby into neglecting the necessary precautionary measures.

Such behaviour is always open to variant interpretations. For instance, many gentle creatures find it painful to have to recognize that this world in which they find themselves is one in which there appears to be little natural correlation between merit and reward, and in which Right and Justice triumph in the end if they happen to be stronger, but not otherwise. Whether you consider this trait a lovable characteristic, or whether you call it half-baked sentimentality, depends on your own view. It seems to me to be both. Of course, we can make a much harsher judgement of such persons by pointing out that the refusal to admit the unpalatable truths relieves them from any twinges of conscience at continuing to live in comfort without doing anything to make things better.

Many similar instances will occur to you from your observation, of yourself as well as of others, of the same sort of thing in the particular opinions and decisions of daily life. The actual ways in which our emotions and feelings and impulses and interests affect what we select for attention, and affect how we group what we do select, are beyond counting in their variety. In the examples we have considered so far, the emotional and other impulses and needs concerned are consciously experienced or are at least near the conscious level. That is to say, the examples we have considered have been instances of selecting and grouping in ways which satisfy, or at least avoid grossly frustrating, various emotional and other impulses and needs which are consciously experienced or are near the conscious level. There are in us, however, other and deeper emotional and other impulses and needs of which we are not conscious, but which profoundly and substantially affect our ways of selecting and grouping, and our ways of behaving. These deep emotional and other impulses and needs are probably much more influential in making us what we are and do than are those of which we are conscious. Indeed it appears to be largely the interplay of these unconscious wishes, impulses and the like, their conflicts and resolutions, which constitute each man's individual personality. This involves us in the subject called by psychologists 'psycho-dynamics', and is a matter for later reading. I am here only concerned to point out that our ways of selecting and grouping are not determined by logical considerations alone, but are assisted or impeded by our feelings, our emotions, our interests, and our impulses, whether we are aware of them or not.

I hope you will now see a little more clearly why I was so insistent that knowing and the increasing of knowledge are not passive processes, but are active processes requiring the expenditure of effort. Considerable effort is often required to overcome the obstruction arising from emotions and feelings and interests. In extreme cases, where the way of 'selecting' and 'grouping' that would give truth would be disturbing to an unbearable degree, the person in question may 'select' and 'group' to form a little subsection of his experience all by itself, which is *within itself* simple, coherent, and comfortable, but which is altogether incoherent with the rest of his experience. This is a very easy and comfortable way of escaping the distress of recognizing the painful situation, but the penalty for doing this is incapacity to co-operate with other people in the daily affairs of life, i.e. the person in question has escaped the pain of admitting the embarrassing facts, but only at the expense of becoming insane. In every asylum in the country there are, for instance, some patients who are there because in the normal way of life they could not satisfy their desire for a position of eminence among their fellows. This desire may rest on the need to overcome some deep-rooted feeling of inferiority, or on some other cause. The outcome is that they are unable to stand the strain of not possessing such eminence, and have got rid of the sense of failure by refusing to admit the facts. Even in the asylum they do this by regarding the asylum as their own property, and by talking to doctors and others as a charming local magnate would talk to visitors whom he is pleased to allow to walk in his grounds and enjoy the gardens. Such insane persons 'select' and 'group' in ways which will enable them to do this, and they refuse to admit the existence of those factors in the situation, such as their inability to get out of the grounds, which are incompatible with the way of 'selecting' and 'grouping' which is comfortable and satisfying for them.

The functional insanities are very extreme cases

of a man's 'selecting' and 'grouping' in ways which enable him to avoid facing facts or recognizing internal conflicts which would disturb and distress him. The 'neuroses' are milder cases, while the same tendency in very minor and quite normal degree shows itself from hour to hour in the lives of all of us.

It is only in exceptional instances that we are aware of the ways in which our emotions and feelings and impulses and interests affect the ways in which we act. Sometimes by our own introspection we can lay bare for ourselves what is going on beneath the surface. Many of the 'spiritual exercises' and analyses of motive urged upon the faithful by the spiritual directors of the Christian Church and by some psychologists are directed towards this end. In most cases, however, it is quite impossible for the individual to do this for himself. The deeps are too deep. It is in such cases sometimes possible for an experienced investigator to discover what is going on beneath the surface. This is what is done, or attempted with varying degrees of success, through various complex techniques by psychoanalysts.

What they thus bring up to the light of day is often alarming and disconcerting, even disgusting, to those to whom this side of life is new, because it results in making very clear that though we have become men and women we have not thereby ceased to be animals. In the breasts of all of us, far below the level of consciousness, there still lie the primordial tiger and the primordial ape, and, perhaps more dangerous to the survival of complex human society, the primordial ass.

All the preceding psychological matters can be followed up in later reading. The point of mentioning them here is to emphasize the complexities of the knowing process, and to give some interim notion of what these complexities are.

To sum up, it appears that in knowing we are 'selecting' and 'grouping' some small scraps of the vast mass of influences that surround us, being driven on to do so by our emotions, feelings, impulses, and interests. We are doing so, or trying to do so, in the simplest and most coherent ways available, but our search for the most simple and coherent ways is perpetually obstructed or reinforced by our emotions, feelings, impulses, and interests, mostly without our recognizing them, so that on the whole we tend to 'select' and 'group' in ways which fall between two extremes, on the one hand the most simple and coherent, and on the other hand the most comfortable. Just how far they fall towards the one extreme or towards the other depends on what sort of persons we are, and on what sort of persons we would wish to be.

CHAPTER X

The Way Forward

THIS book was written to produce an effect upon the reader. It was not intended as an exposition of a philosophical position. It will as a by-product have suggested one, but its main purpose was to produce a certain effect upon the interested or potentially interested reader, and if it produces that effect it will have served its specific and limited purpose. It will have done so even if, in later years, the reader does not remember very much of what he read in it, and even if he forgets that he ever read it at all. The effective is not necessarily the memorable.

The first element in the intended effect was that after working through these preceding nine chapters, whether he agrees with them or not, the reader should begin to know from his own experience what it feels like to think philosophically.

The second, and perhaps the more important, element in the intended effect was to produce that state of mind which the first impact of philosophy always produces upon the competent reader, namely a certain freshness of outlook, mingled throughout with a very much heightened feeling of general intellectual insecurity and uncertainty. This is essential. Unless this feeling of uncertainty as to what can really be depended upon as a basis for our knowledge and belief has, at this stage, been created in the reader, the book will have failed in one of its purposes. This state of uncertainty and insecurity is not one in which it is either necessary or desirable to loiter, but it is a stage on our way to intellectual emancipation through which we must all pass. Unless we do experience a period in which we feel vividly insecure and uncertain as to the bases on which our beliefs and opinions rest, we are unlikely ever to emerge from the condition of thinking and acting within limits laid down by unsatisfactory presuppositions of whose existence we are unaware. This period of bewildered insecurity will pass, but it will leave as its permanent after-effect a general intellectual wariness, and this will in time become a quality of character as well as of intellect.

The effects outlined above are those which were produced upon me, to my continuing gratitude, by the first lectures on philosophy that I ever heard, and I can only hope that this book will produce something of the same effect upon you.

The by-product referred to above was that the reader should be brought to understand the practical as well as theoretical importance of the theory of knowledge, that is to say, the importance of the assumptions or views we hold as to the nature of knowledge, and should be offered for his consideration a working hypothesis which is markedly different from, and I believe better than, that which he had previously tacitly assumed. Part of the reason for this is that the very contrast serves to make the existence of the previous tacit assumptions more clear, but the topic is important in itself, because, for the reasons outlined in Chapter II, what we think about it lays down limits within which we are confined in our thinking about everything else. It has therefore an importance and influence that is unique and supreme. The suggested working hypothesis will, I believe, liberate the reader from some serious misunderstandings, and from the practical inconveniences consequent thereon, provided of course that he does not merely accept unquestioningly what I say, but makes it his own by thinking it over for himself. The suggested hypothesis is no more than suggested, but it may serve the reader in the meantime until he achieves a fuller liberation for himself by further reading and thinking.

You will now want to read further and pass beyond the merely introductory stage at which we stand. Some readers may find it profitable to go over the whole book again from the beginning and to detect in so doing how much their outlook has changed since they looked upon its pages for the first time. Others will want to go on at once to wider questions than those here discussed. The topic which has been our subject, namely the theory of knowledge, certainly has a supreme importance, for the reasons given above, but it is only one among the many topics that come under the name of philosophy, and it is probably not the one that springs most readily to mind at the mention of that name. There are other topics also which a student of philosophy expects to have brought to his notice. This chapter consists of notes on the principal among these topics, with advice as to further reading.

We are all familiar with the names ' metaphysics ', ' ethics ', ' psychology ', ' logic ', ' theology '. These names have in course of time come to be adopted because the particular studies which they designate have at least the appearance of being comparatively independent, and hence of deserving the dignity of special names of their own. The alleged independence of these various inquiries is, however, largely spurious. They cannot be pursued adequately in isolation one from another. They overlap, and findings reached in one may radically affect findings in others. Still, subject to that considerable qualification, certain rough working distinctions of topics can be made, and these in fact are made and are regularly employed in the literature of philosophy. The principal of these are as follows. The general inquiry into the nature of the universe and man's place in it is usually and conveniently called ' metaphysics ', though the very derivation of that name shows in itself how vague these titles are. It is derived from Greek words meaning literally 'that which comes after physics'. This is sometimes understood as meaning the inquiry which goes beyond physics, but the name in fact arose in quite a different way. Aristotle wrote a book on 'physics', which was called by that name, and also a book on general philosophical problems. This latter book had at first no title, because no name for the subject then existed. The early editors of Aristotle placed this book after the 'physics' in the copies of his writings which they had made by the scribes, and in consequence the book became known as 'that which comes after the physics' or, in Greek, the 'metaphysics', and so in course of time the subject itself came to be known as 'metaphysics'. Philosophers who are dubious of the associations of the name 'metaphysics' commonly refer to this type of study simply as 'general philosophy'.

Then there is 'moral philosophy'. The inquiry into what things are most worth while in life, and what things are really rather footling in spite of all the fuss made about them, and into other similar problems concerning right and wrong, good and bad, constitutes the subject usually called 'ethics' or 'moral philosophy', these being respectively Greek and Latin names for the inquiry into ways and standards of behaviour, and into what is meant by 'standards' and 'ideals'.

Again let me emphasize that these names are merely somewhat indefinite labels used for practical convenience. There is no separate and independent inquiry corresponding to each separate and independent name. For instance, the question of what constitutes the zest of life, and what standards men are to live by—a problem now acute on the passing of specifically religious beliefs and standards from large masses of men — is one of many questions which involve metaphysics and ethics and psychology, and also theology, in any attempt at an answer.

The subject called 'psychology' is notoriously difficult to define, though we all understand more or less what sorts of subjects are investigated by psychologists. The principal importance of their work for us in the present connexion is the light it can throw on the ways in which the opinions we reach and retain or reject are affected by what we conveniently call 'psychological' factors, that is to say by considerations in ourselves, conscious or unconscious, as distinct from the evidence in question. A considerably deepened understanding of these matters is coming from recent advances in psychology and psychoanalysis, especially from advances in what is now coming to be called 'psycho-dynamics', to which reference is made later among the books suggested for further reading. In this connexion there is some need of a special warning. The work being done is obviously of considerable value, but some of the conclusions reached appear to be based on insufficient evidence. In spite of this, the conclusions *may* be true. The investigators may on these points be intuitive geniuses. On the other hand they may on these points be unscientific eccentrics leaping to conclusions. There is as yet insufficient evidence to warrant a confident conclusion one way or the other. It is worth labouring this warning here in order to guard against two opposite tendencies which the extreme pronouncements of many contemporary psychologists and psychoanalysts evoke in their readers, namely, on the one hand the uncritical tendency to accept everything they say, and on the other hand the equally undiscriminating tendency to disbelieve the whole on finding some particular point unbelievable. You will probably find both these tendencies in yourself if you go on to read the two books on the subject recommended later in the chapter.

As to the subject called 'theology', the common view is muddled, and requires clarification. There is a common belief among the non-religious that the views of the theologians are irrelevant to modern conditions and may safely be disregarded. This is not so. The theologians are men who, like the philosophers, attempt to find out what sort of universe this is, and what sort of beings we are who inhabit it. Unlike the philosophers, however, who give innumerably different kinds of answers, the theologians give answers which in one respect are of one kind only, namely answers that assume throughout the existence of God. The theologians explain the universe, and ourselves and our situation, by the theory that the universe has been created by or is dependent upon a God or Gods (some different groups of theologians have different views as to which); and that it is divinely planned and conditioned (some different groups of theologians have different views as to whether this plan bears any relation to the purposes and ideals of men); and that men are creaturely beings (some different groups of theologians have different views as to the relation in which these creaturely beings stand to their Creator); and that a man in consequence ought to regulate his life in accordance with these considerations (some different groups of theologians have different views as to how this should be done).

The question for us is not whether the matters discussed by the theologians are important. About this point there is no doubt. These matters are supremely important. The question is whether what the theologians say about them is true. The doctrine of original sin, for instance, is an estimate, expressed no doubt in language which the layman may find a little strange, of human nature. The question for us is whether it is a sound estimate or not, and this is a question of the highest importance. A radically different estimate of human nature was produced and preached by many other thinkers, for instance by Rousseau and his followers, and by some theologians mainly of the lesser sects. They maintained that men are naturally good, and that all natural impulses are essentially good and lead to harm only when thwarted. The truth or otherwise of these contradictory estimates is of profound practical importance. For instance, the acceptance of the ' original sin ' estimate in an extreme form leads to that morbid and distasteful puritanism which still lingers and disfigures the lives of many otherwise admirable people, while the adoption of Rousseau's estimate in an extreme form leads to public disorder and personal unhappiness, and to the development of types of character so futile as hardly to be worth calling characters at all.

These topics are interesting and most important, but they are not for discussion here. They are referred to here only to illustrate the point that the questions discussed by the theologians are important, whether we agree or not with the answers given by them.

A further word of explanation is required as to the common assumption that there is a conflict between science and theology. This is a mis-statement of a conflict which is real and profound, but is of a different kind. There is not, and cannot be, any conflict between views on scientific matters and theological views, because they are views about different subjects. But there is a very real and profound conflict between the account of the universe and of man's place in it which is given by the theologians, and the account of the universe and of man's place in it which is given by most scientists. It is an observable fact that most scientists tend to a somewhat materialistic or at least non-theological view of man and the universe, but this view is not itself a scientific view. It is one kind of metaphysical theory, which happens to be held for understandable reasons by most scientists, but it is not a scientific theory on that account, any more than it would be a financial theory if it were held by a stockbroker. The situation is that the theologian has worked out, or assumed, one answer to the problem of man and his nature, namely a general philosophical view characterized by reference to a God or Gods as an explanation, while the scientist has worked out, or assumed, a different general philosophical view, usually characterized by material explanations only.

It may be, as some argue, that theology merely represents an explanation of the universe which certain types of mind find congenial owing to deep psychological causes. It may be that the discontents and depravities of men which the theologians attempt to understand by studying the relationship in which the individual stands to God can be adequately understood only by studying the relationship in which the individual stands to other men in the texture of complex society. It may be that the theologians have simply made a mistake, and that the problems for which they proffer personal religion as an answer can be properly dealt with only in terms of social psychology. This may or may not be so. I do not think that the matter is so simple, but, whatever the answer, these are wider problems not for discussion here. The point that I am using this instance to emphasize is that the theologians, or some of them, have something to say which is worth paying attention to. The theology of Christianity and other religions does admittedly express much human egotism and self-preoccupation, but it, or some part of it, also represents a vast accumulation of human wisdom, and of evidence about, if not always insight into, the restless and unsatisfied heart of man.

The subject called ' logic ' is generally reckoned a part of philosophy, and as such deserves to be studied.

In this connection, it is well to bear in mind how this subject developed during the twenty-four centuries through which it has existed as an essential of the higher education of Western Europe. If you were to accept unquestioningly the common assumption about the nature of language discussed in chapter IX, and were in consequence to accept unquestioningly the assumption that there exist self-complete units of meaning which are either true or false in themselves, then you could create a new subject of inquiry by analysing the inner structure of these alleged units, and by examining the relations in which they could stand to other such units in the building up of complex arguments. This was done with painstaking and somewhat humourless industry by Greek, medieval, and later logicians. In this way there developed the traditional formal logic, and in course of time its modern derivatives.[1] As yet there is no general recognition that formal logic and its modern derivatives are based on the above assumption about the nature of language and meaning, and the teaching of it still survives in some universities as a kind of intellectual fossil. However, even though the traditional logic is based on an erroneous assumption (which is one reason, though only one, for the distrust which so many men and women feel and express for 'logic'), some study of it is well worth while, because without some knowledge of that subject it is impossible to understand either the thought of medieval times or such thought of modern times as is based on medieval thought. This is important, because the latter is much larger in proportion than is commonly recognized.

These names, 'metaphysics', 'ethics', 'theology', 'logic', 'psychology', are the labels most commonly used for the various main subjects, or main aspects

[1] Including that curious contemporary hybrid of the modern and archaic called Logical Positivism.

of the same subject, into which men have inquired under the general title of philosophy. You will now yourself find, I hope, after having been brought to this stage by this Introduction, that your own interests are themselves leading you forward to inquire further on these lines.

To go on and carry out these further and deeper inquiries for oneself is extremely difficult. This is, therefore, where the professional philosophers make or ought to make their contribution. Most people are too fully preoccupied with the moment to moment exigencies of daily life to have time to give continuous thought to such inquiries, even if they have the interest and ability to do so. The social function of the philosopher in the community, as I see it, is to carry out the labour of such inquiries as best he can according to his ability and opportunity, and to pass on his considered conclusions in assimilable form to the rest of the community, as his return for being left free to think in modest comfort and comparative peace. Professional philosophers will here remark somewhat sourly that this is an idealization of their lot. The best of them, those who in the end develop as well as merely transmit the philosophical inheritance, are usually though by no means always possessed of some degree of administrative ability and of the impulse to exercise it, and their philosophic seclusion is in consequence a remote ideal which they only intermittently achieve. This, however, is not a disadvantage except in extreme cases, since without the congested experience thus accumulated they would have little upon which to philosophize when the opportunity of quiet did come. Philosophizing in the absence of adequate experience produces worthless philosophy. In every generation, unfortunately, there crop up professional philosophers who do this. It is observable that men may become philosophers either by intensity of interest in philosophy, or by comparative deficiency of interest in other sides of life. It is the latter type who provoke the fully justified comment that there is no opinion so wild, and contrary to the common experience of men, but some philosopher has held it. Admittedly, even philosophical conclusions worthy of the name may look at first glance very different from common sense. Indeed they nearly always do so, owing to their being profound, which makes them difficult, and new, which makes them more difficult, but examination shows them to be in fact only the outcome of common-sense inquiry tenaciously pursued beyond the point at which most men drop off because it becomes too difficult. The professional philosopher has more opportunity than most men to meditate in quiet on the experiences he shares with his fellows. In return it is, or ought to be, his function to provide some sort of working hypothesis about the universe and man's place in it, which will enable his generation to cope a little more successfully with the extremely adverse conditions of human existence against which the better part of mankind contends with so much quiet gallantry.

This philosophical preoccupation involves some very definite disadvantages. To go thus ' voyaging through strange seas of thought, alone ', is not suited to all temperaments, and many who have tried it have collapsed under the starkness of it. Thinking is a dangerous trade. It is also a troublesome one, as the thinker while he is thinking is apt to be an unsociable nuisance to his family and his friends, and in consequence to himself.

The professional philosophers are well aware that they have been unable to perform their social function with any high degree of adequacy. Still, the reading of their works will greatly help you, and with them you will have to be philosophically content, for they are the best help you can ever get.

In the light of the preceding, my advice to you on what to read next is as follows. By 'read next' I mean literally 'read next'. The books mentioned are books which the man or woman who has worked through this Introduction will find both possible and profitable to read now.

As the next stage in metaphysics, or general philosophy, you can if you wish read Descartes and Locke and Berkeley, and so follow in detail the run of the argument outlined in chapters III to VII, but if I were you I would as my next step go forward to a more ambitious project and read A. N. Whitehead's[1] *Adventures of Ideas* (Cambridge University Press, and also obtainable, paper-covered, in the Pelican series). Much of it is difficult reading, but it opens wide vistas.

You will also want to begin ethics or moral philosophy. The best way I know of to do this is to read J. S. Mill's *Utilitarianism* and Kant's *Fundamental Principles of the Metaphysic of Morals* (both obtainable in various editions).

As an introduction to theology, I suggest that you read Kirsopp Lake's *Paul, his Heritage and Legacy* (Christophers).

As to formal logic, you will find the essentials, and no more than the essentials, in my *Traditional Formal Logic* (Methuen).

On the ways in which our feelings and interests obstruct, or distort, or facilitate, or even make possible, our understanding, the psychologists have produced innumerable books of very diversified quality. You would find a convenient and very brief first introduction to the subject in Geraldine Coster's

---

[1] Alfred North Whitehead (1861–   ). Mathematician, and joint author with Bertrand Russell of *Principia Mathematica*. Later turned to philosophy and produced a series of most influential books of which *Adventures of Ideas* is the most accessible to the non-technical reader.

Psycho-analysis for Normal People (Oxford University Press). A considerably fuller and more up-to-date study is given in J. P. Brown's *Psychodynamics of Abnormal Behaviour* (McGraw-Hill), which is much more readable and illuminating than its somewhat alarming title suggests.

What to advise on the reading of the Greek philosophers is a difficult problem. An assumption underlying most of the Greek philosophy accessible in English translation is that there exist two worlds, a real and permanent world known only to the intellect, and a changing, unreal world known by the senses. For reasons which will be clear to the reader of this book, this view, though historically understandable, appears to me thoroughly wrong-headed. It does, however, represent an ancient and continuous philosophical tradition which moulded and largely still moulds the habits of mind of educated Europeans. I should therefore suggest your reading Plato's *Symposium* and *Phaedo*, and then his *Republic*, in any of the easily obtainable translations. Lowes Dickinson's *Greek View of Life* (Methuen) is a standard descriptive introduction to that interpretation of Greek life and philosophy which has been most influential in English education.

The above books will themselves suggest further reading, both in the greater philosophers and in contemporary writers, to any extent you wish to undertake.